Life After Loss

A Journey Into Wholeness

Life After Loss

A Journey Into Wholeness

Dorn J.B. Wheatley

Treasure House

An Imprint of
Destiny Image, Inc.®
P.O. Box 310
Shippensburg, PA 17257-0310

"For where your treasure is
there will your heart be also." Matthew 6:21

ISBN 1-56043-842-8

For Worldwide Distribution
Printed in the U.S.A.

Treasure House books are available through these fine distributors outside the United States:

Christian Growth, Inc.
Jalan Kilang-Timor, Singapore 0315

Vine Christian Centre
Mid Glamorgan, Wales, United Kingdom

Rhema Ministries Trading
Randburg, South Africa

Vision Resources
Ponsonby, Auckland, New Zealand

Salvation Book Centre
Petaling, Jaya, Malaysia

WA Buchanan Company
Geebung, Queensland, Australia

Successful Christian Living
Capetown, Rep. of South Africa

Word Alive
Niverville, Manitoba, Canada

Inside the U.S., call toll free to order:
1-800-722-6774

Dedication

To my daughter, Tesa, who at this critical stage of her life (adolescence) needs desperately to find and to grasp hold of her identity to ultimately become a whole woman. You too have lost, but you will become whole.

To my mother, Jean Bertrand Henry; my mother-in-law, Angel Wheatley; my niece, Cherise Hodge; my sisters Velma and Roslyn; my sisters-in-law Roxanne and Luana; and the other women in my family—together we have shared the pain. Let us all move forward with renewed vigor toward a bright future that is not hindered by our past.

To every female who has sensed a void in an area of her life formerly filled with love, peace, joy, notable self-esteem, integrity, or perhaps a relationship with her Creator.

To every male who has also had to contend with loss. Life has also taught me that contrary to popular belief, men hurt too!

Finally, to those who long for the aforementioned qualities (love, peace, joy, notable self-esteem, integrity, and ultimately right standing with God) that constitute wholeness.

Women, let us give birth to our wholeness! Woe unto us if we remain with child. Let us give birth so that we can exemplify wholeness to our families, and ultimately, wholeness to the world!

*Men, your wholeness is equally important. While the dictates of a "politically correct" society assume that males are not **feelers**, always be mindful that your **Life After Loss** is directly or indirectly affecting everyone around you, either positively or negatively. If you choose wholeness, everybody wins.*

Acknowledgments

I thank my Father God who made it possible for me to be reconciled to Him by sending His Son Jesus to this earth.

I thank Jesus Christ who loves me and has freed me from my sins by His blood and has made me a part of His royal race to serve His Father—I give Him glory, honor, and praise.

Holy Spirit, I thank You for wisdom, knowledge, understanding, counsel, power, and reverential and obedient fear of the Lord. You kept Your promise and stayed with me throughout this book.

Tesa, thank you for your example of what God said in Matthew 18:3. Unless we become like children, we will never enter into the Kingdom of Heaven. Thank you for your patience and understanding while I spent many hours writing this book. You were always there, willing and ready, to provide paper and a pen when I became inspired to write. Thank you for your support. I love you much!

My pastor, Reverend Charles Phillips, thank you for your dedication to this project, for writing the Foreword, and for your commitment to help me develop and fulfill my God-given purpose.

Special thanks also to Debra Bivins for editing this book. Debbie, I will be forever grateful for your kindness and encouraging words. Your cheery personality and bright beautiful smile added a special touch to this work.

Special thanks to Delores Armour who interceded and stood in the gap during one of the most critical times in my life. Sister Armour, when God asked for someone to stand in the gap, I believe that you were the first to say "Lord, here I am; send me." I thank God for your commitment toward His service.

Special thanks to Judith Bennett for staying by my side and allowing herself to be a vessel for God to use to express the gift of exhortation in its purest form. Judy, thanks for the encouragement and support, but most of all, thanks for the shoulder that you loaned me to shed many tears. I love you Judy; joy came in the morning!

Contents

Foreword

By death, divorce, abandonment, rejection, or any other of life's occasional cruelties, it hurts to lose. The sense of loss is difficult to articulate in that its intangibility is relative.

Paul states in Second Corinthians 1:8, "…that we were pressed out of measure…." As this great apostle tried to express the depth of his despair, there was no way to measure it. There was just the sense of pleasure exhausted. The unfortunate part of passing this way is that many feel destined to remain at this station in life.

If you are one of those who "arrive at this address," you have several options open to you. The choice you make will determine your future.

The Bible has always spoken highly of widows and others who have experienced loss. There was always a conscientious concern for the well-being of these persons—from Ruth to the discussion of neglected widows in Acts 6. Jesus Himself gives the comforting words to all who have had to face a loss of any kind, "I will never leave you or forsake you."

Those who will be privileged to turn the pages of this book will take an *all-important journey* with a young widow who ultimately made the right choices that led her to the healing and wholeness she enjoys today.

This author is very bright and articulate, yet very private. It is, in fact, a sovereign act of God that has brought forth these words to these pages.

Dorn has opened a very personal room in her life to see to it that others will benefit from her journey. I trust that when you come to the end of this book, you will likewise make a remarkable discovery—*a healed you!*

Pastor Charles Phillips
Liberty Temple
African Methodist
Episcopal Zion Church
Washington, D.C.

Introduction

My husband's death began a series of tragedies that left me feeling trapped in an enormous storm with gigantic whirlwinds. The hurt that I experienced from these tragedies initiated a domino-like effect, which appeared to have no end. My life headed in a downward direction until I came to the realization that the only true answer was to confront the root cause of the toppling dominos. Therefore with great fervor, I pressed toward freedom.

Today, the storm has passed; all calm has been restored; and new peace now overwhelms my soul! This peace is like a palm tree planted firmly, its roots reaching deep. Although this palm tree may sway back and forth as new storms arise, they will not be strong enough to uproot it or break its stature.

The objective of this book is to provide you with simple, clear, experiential, and proven guidance for confronting your pain, moving through the healing process, and emerging in absolute wholeness! Yes, achieving a state of wholeness is indeed possible! *I have come to realize that wholeness is not only possible, but it is critical if we plan to survive in what I believe is the last day hour.*

As we move closer to the twenty-first century, it is becoming more and more critical that we persevere through the healing process. *I believe that it is crucial for us to acknowledge who we are and move forward in absolute wholeness—a valiant state that will empower us to survive in this world of increasing darkness.* If we are honest with ourselves, we will admit that the hurts and weights of this world are creating burdens that are bringing many people to a point of despondency. Therefore, let us make the decision now to boldly confront the ills in our lives, move forward, and experience the abundant life of God's Kingdom here on earth as it is in Heaven!

The devil is on a rampage today, diligently seeking whomever he may devour, and he is actively trying to establish his kingdom of darkness. I believe that the enemy's strategy is to destroy our future by attacking our future leaders and ambassadors both spiritually and naturally.

Nonetheless, the world is waiting for us to manifest as sons of God who will hold up the light for this dying world. Not only is the world waiting for us to manifest as sons of God, but we ourselves, who have the first fruits of the Spirit, groan inwardly for our adoption as sons, the redemption of our bodies (see Rom. 8:23). Our inner man will never have peace until we put aside all our fleshly weights and become who God has intended us to be. Jesus has made us kings and priests unto God (see Rev. 1:6). Kings and priests, I dare you to take your position and walk in authority!

I owe God my very life because of the inexpressible love that He bestowed upon me through His Son Jesus Christ. So, it is for His name's sake (God the Father, God the Son, and God the Holy Spirit) that I have written this book. *Lord, may You be glorified and revealed in the hearts of Your people. I pray that Your healing virtues will become evident to every individual reading this book. May Your Holy Spirit flow through the words on each page and fill every reader's heart. Lord Jesus, may You increase as I decrease.*

Chapter 1

My Story

Tragedy struck suddenly and without warning. It destroyed the perfect world I called "my life." At the age of 23, I learned the meaning of loss, loneliness, despair, and brokenness. Stu was gone. My life, as I knew it, was over. Still numb from shock and thankful for a few moments of solitude, I slipped into the bedroom as my thoughts raced back over the years. Like a child struggling to pick up the pieces of a broken treasure, I gathered my precious memories, one by one, refusing to allow anyone or anything to take them from me.

I closed my eyes and could almost feel his arms around me again. He was my safety, my strength. We were so much a part of each other. I missed his laughter and playfulness. Oh, how I needed to hear him tease and laugh again...my hands reached for the family photo album...I turned one page after another until my eyes focused on a picture of Tesa and her dad. They used to have such good times together. What is this going to do to her life? What am I going to say to my precious little girl? As much as I wanted to hold her in my arms, I was *thankful that I did not have to bear the burden of explanations and tender smiles right now.*

Steuart (Stu) H. Wheatley and I met shortly after my sixteenth birthday. My best friend introduced us, and although I did not fall in love with him immediately, his gentleness and kind ways soon won me over. Steuart lived a clean simple life, and this attracted me to him. First we were friends, then brother and sister, and a few years later, husband and wife. He became my first love.

It did not matter that I was nine years younger than Stu. His incredibly unselfish ways allowed me to grow and mature with him. Life with Stu was so exciting. We just enjoyed doing things together. We fished, hiked, hunted birds, and played sports together.

We anticipated our daughter Tesa's birth around January 15 in 1982. Oh, what a surprise it was to have her show up three weeks early on December 25. She was a true Christmas gift! We quickly made the adjustment and moved into the next phase of our lives—parenthood. This was a real challenge for me. Steuart, however, was the perfect dad (definitely a "Mr. Mom"). I was so fortunate to have him, and I often reminded myself that our relationship was too good to be true.

I started college when Tesa was only eight months old. Oh, the responsibilities! Sometimes they were overwhelming. College and family life often conflicted. I usually dropped Tesa off at the babysitter about 7:30 a.m. each day before my classes started. Stu picked her up at 3:30 p.m. Some days I did not get home from school until 9:00 p.m. On those late evenings, I arrived home to find Tesa bathed, fed, tucked in bed, and a hot meal waiting for me.

On other days, Stu kept Tesa occupied as I locked myself away to study for an exam or to read the assigned chapters for class the next day. I used to hear them laughing and playing in the next room. I would smile and think, *At least Tesa has her dad, and he's so good with her.* I continually promised her, "Tesa, I will be finished with school before your fifth birthday." She listened and eagerly waited for me to resume my motherhood responsibilities on a full-time basis.

On Christmas and summer breaks, I always made up the lost moments by spending extra time with both of them. Even though I felt like we had the model family, "something" seemed to be missing. I could not put my finger on it. Maybe we needed God in our lives? Perhaps we needed our own home? Or maybe we needed more children?

We wanted all of these things and more. Steuart and I bought land, and we planned to custom build our own home after I graduated. We both wanted to have more children. We also planned to start attending church after I finished college. It seemed like such a short time to wait and all of our reasons for waiting seemed logical.

I was so proud of the fact that I would be able to contribute to my family's future after I had earned my college degree. A mother at 18, I had definitely beaten all the odds, and my life was better than I ever imagined.

Stu worked very hard at his job and at home, but he seemed to need space and time with his friends. His annual vacation was a highlight for him. He enjoyed fishing, hunting birds, and even playing some basketball. This renewed his enthusiasm and gave him the drive to continue his demanding schedule. Although I missed him, I tried real hard to understand his need for rejuvenation.

Stu had looked forward to his October vacation for a long time, and He had talked about it all summer. I tried to convince him to take his vacation in August instead of October because I had the summer off from school. I loved my husband's company, but by October I would be engrossed in my fall semester classes. He did not want to change the date, so I decided to live with it. *Why Stu? Why didn't you change that date?*

October finally came and so did the time for Stu to relax and have some fun. He was so excited the night before. He unloaded the fishing and hunting gear and spent most of the evening talking about his plans for the next day. Tesa watched him organize the tackle box, fishing rods, and all the other hunting equipment. They were so cute together. His enthusiasm reminded me of a school child the day before summer break. After watching them for a few minutes, I returned to my books. Well into my fall semester, I had a major test scheduled for the next day.

Yes, I had to stay home and study if I planned to pass that test. It was just one of the prices that needed to be paid. Steuart woke up early the next morning, about 5:30 a.m. He woke me with a kiss, "I'm about ready to leave. I have to catch some sprats [a small fish often used for fishing bait] before they leave with the morning tide. I'll be home in time to drop you off at school for your exam tonight."

The cloudy sky looked as though a great storm might be coming in. I took another glance out the window just before he left home. The weather had not improved and I was a little concerned, but I knew that he had waited for this day too long for me to say anything except, "Be careful, Stu, watch the weather."

He smiled, kissed me, and gathered up the last of his fishing and hunting gear, "Good-bye, see you later." I heard the sound of his jeep as he drove out of our driveway, not knowing that this would be the very last time that I would see him.

The tears started spilling from my eyes again. They refused to stop. His kiss, his voice, the sound of his jeep; they all seemed only moments away instead of a lifetime. Something inside of me wanted to stop gathering these memories, but I knew I had to go on. I needed to keep every one of them just as close to me as I could. The telephone rang in the next room, but I heard it only faintly. My thoughts were in another place, at another time, and I did not want to leave them, even for a moment.

After Stu left, I stayed home and studied intensely for the five o'clock exam. Grandma had taken Tesa to kindergarten, and I expected Stu to bring her home at 3:30 p.m., which left plenty of time for me to get to college. I sat patiently waiting for Stu until four o'clock. *What happened? Stu's never late...I can't ever remember him being late, not even once,* I wondered to myself.

A funny feeling stirred inside of me and an uneasiness moved me to respond to it. I called Tesa's school to see if her dad had picked her up. No, Stu had not shown up and she was still at school waiting for him. A few moments later the telephone rang and a police officer informed me, "Mrs. Wheatley, there's been an accident."

"What...what do you mean?"

"I'm very sorry that I have to tell you this, but your husband has accidently drowned..." His voice trailed off in the distance. I could not comprehend the meaning of the officer's words. I felt as though my life had turned into a movie; or rather, this was only a nightmare that I had to wake up from.

"No, not Stu! Not my husband; you must be mistaken!" The officer returned a few words of consolation through the cold telephone, but I did not hear them. I mumbled a response and then the dull buzz of the dial tone sounded in my ear. October 21, 1986, my husband, Steuart Wheatley, was dead. My entire world, one that I had put so much faith in, started to slip away from me. I could not do anything to stop it. One day everything was perfect and the next day....

Lying there in my bedroom after Stu's memorial service, I wanted to die. There wasn't anything left to live for. All the memories, the pieces of my life, the good times and the bad; life as I knew it was gone. I heard a knock at the front door and I prayed for it to stop, but the intruding sound persisted. Slowly, I rose from my thoughts and my solitude to greet my guests.

Thoughts of dying and hopelessness returned again and again over the next few months. My husband's death was only the beginning of a series of devastating events and heartaches in my life. Four days later my father's brother (Uncle Emanuel) also died suddenly from a heart attack. A month later, a $150,000 lawsuit was filed against me for a traffic incident that had occurred two years earlier. Lastly, I learned that my oldest sister was terminally ill with cancer. She finally died seven months later.

I cried uncontrollably for weeks. I was not a born-again Christian, but I did believe in God. I prayed for understanding and questioned God again and again. The loss in my life was too great to comprehend. It happened too suddenly. Everything and everyone on this earth had let me down.

People tried to comfort me, but I refused their gestures of compassion, even though they meant well. The only voice I listened to was my own. *No one understands my distress…this pain is just too hard for me to bear…I can't go on without Stu.*

Yes, I still had Tesa and I loved her dearly. Sometimes we held on to each other tightly without speaking, sharing a pain too deep for words. Other times, however, the pain in my heart numbed my ability to respond to anyone, even Tesa. Although I knew she needed her mother, I felt incapable of being the mother I had been. In addition to my grief, feelings of failure, defeat, and helplessness swept through me every time I looked at my beautiful little girl. How will I ever explain this tragedy to Tesa? How do you explain such anguish and heartache to a four year old when you can't even explain them to yourself. I loved Tesa dearly, and my greatest fear was that Tesa felt as much pain as I did. I was losing my mind over this dilemma, and I feared that my little girl would never experience a normal life. However, I held onto the fact that our love for each other would ultimately bring us through this tragedy.

I began to deteriorate really fast, and I missed a lot of school. Even though I only had a few weeks left, I saw no reason to continue. My motivation for life was gone. Stu had been the center of our life together.

Everyone tried to support me. Some of my classmates came together and talked me into finishing my last few weeks of school. "At least do it for your daughter's sake," they encouraged me. Not long after that, I realized that I had to think about Tesa and stop feeling sorry for myself. I had to press forward, at least for my little girl. I went back to school, but I cannot remember how I concentrated long enough to comprehend the subject matter. I finally finished school and found a job in the field of accounting.

God was with me long before I realized it. Many Christian students used this opportunity to witness to me. Every day they gave me new Scriptures to read, and many people planted seeds of faith in me. They prayed for me and encouraged me to go on. This in itself made me curious about God. Consequently, I started to attend church, visiting one church after another, searching for answers to my questions.

Church services usually made me cry because I hurt so badly. I wanted someone to cradle me and hug me enough to make the hurt go away like Stu used to do. Instead of receiving strength from the service, I usually spent the time silently crying out to God as the tears streamed down my face. *No one understands what I am going through…these tragedies are just too much to bear…at 23 my life should be just beginning…instead, it's ended. Why, God, why?*

I was not the only one who experienced a loss. Stu's parents had lost their son. My uncle's family had lost him. My immediate family had lost my sister. However, I had lost a husband, an uncle, and a sister. On top of this I had to face a lawsuit. I felt as though my load was heavier than anyone else's and no one seemed to understand.

One day, I reached the point that I cried out to God, "If You don't show up God, I am out of here!" I was on the brink of losing my mind. With that ultimatum, I reached complete brokenness. Not long after that God brought an evangelist to town. He shared the message of salvation and gave me hope. I confessed Jesus Christ as my Savior and my journey to healing and wholeness began.

Selah
(Pause and think about it.)

Recounting the story of my pain has a purpose. Recounting the story of the pain in your life has a purpose too. Imagine a bucket partially filled with dirt. The dirt represents the hurt, disappointment, and pain in our lives. We need to acknowledge the dirt and yield it to God so that He can supernaturally unload the filth. If we do not, whatever solution we add to the dirt will create mud. The mud denotes an obscure life of confusion and darkness.

I came to the point of brokenness and surrender. This is the place that new life begins. Will you take a few moments right now to recount your own story and admit that you cannot do anything to put the pieces back together again? If you have done this, your healing has begun.

Chapter 2

Life After Loss

I will never forget the night I accepted Jesus Christ as my Savior. It was at a revival in a baseball field. When the evangelist gave the altar call, I sprang out of the bleachers and made my way forward through the crowd. That night, a load lifted off of my shoulders, and for the first time in months, I slept peacefully. I began to crave everything that God had to offer, including water baptism and the baptism in the Holy Spirit.

Later I asked myself, *Why did you take so long to realize that Jesus was the answer?* I went from church to church until I found one where I felt comfortable and where the love of God was manifested in the hearts of the people. I felt as though I had arrived and had finally found the perfect life to replace the one I had lost when Stu died.

Life as a new Christian can be exciting. The sky looks brighter and the colors of the earth have more depth. If we are not already accustomed to biblical language, a new world of communication opens up for us.

We learn to talk to other Christians about our God, and we learn to talk to Him in prayer.

As exciting as my new life as a Christian was, I continued to need the security of a neat, orderly world. In many respects, I simply replaced my relationship with Stu with a relationship with God. Stu had always been the glue that held the many factions of my life as a wife, mother, and student together. Now, I expected God to do the same. However, Stu and I had something that God and I did not have yet.

Stu and I had a deep intimate knowledge of each other. This knowledge enabled us to live and work together in harmony, each one complimenting the other. I knew my husband and he knew me. We acknowledged our pain as well as our joy to each other. Our feelings ran very deep, sometimes too deep for words, but we lived together in an honest, knowing relationship that did not have any room for hidden agendas or painful repressions.

My new relationship with God was different. I loved Him and He loved me, but I tried to bury the past, hide the pain, and repress my needs as a woman. In addition, I did not take the time to get to know God the way that He wanted me to know him.

Superficial Christianity Can Be Dangerous

At first, I only concentrated on the superficial goodness of God. If there were easy answers, I found them. If there were convenient solutions for the Christian life,

I used them. These answers were not wrong, but they only offered me a quick-fix, a Band-Aid to cover up the turmoil and pain of losing Stu. Many of them taught me how to *pretend* to be a victorious Christian, without understanding what it really meant to have victory in my life.

I did not take the time to recognize the pain, identify the feelings, and confront the conflict within me. Still wounded and broken from losing my husband, I became overzealous without grasping the full knowledge of God. I believed that I knew everything I needed to know about God and salvation. Self-righteousness and pride took root in my heart and in my life.

Proverbs 16:18 says, "Pride goeth before destruction, and an haughty spirit before a fall." The Bible also says that it is not good to have zeal without knowledge (see Rom. 10:2). I definitely had zeal, but my pride did not allow me to see that in addition to lacking a knowledge of God, I still had a great deal of hurt inside. I refused to admit my weaknesses as a woman and as a Christian to myself and to God. After all, I had been an achiever, and I intended to remain that way.

My flesh had taken full reign over my spirit and was bringing judgment upon me. Too ashamed to admit my problem, I went on in total self-righteousness, living a self-directed life of anxiety that caused me to make many more mistakes and misjudgments.

Isaiah 33:6 says that wisdom and knowledge shall be the stability of our times and the strength of our salvation. As a babe in Christ, trying to live a life of holiness and trying to adjust to the world as a Christian, I needed both wisdom and knowledge.

Unresolved Pain Can Be Destructive

Eight months after Stu's death my employer selected me to go to New Orleans for a week to represent my colleagues at a professional conference. In New Orleans, I met some colleagues from our office headquarters. Although I did not know these individuals personally, I felt a little more secure with them in this strange place. Every day, I hung out with my little group, and I went where they went. My new friends were not Christians and they participated in everything that New Orleans had to offer. The streets were filled with bars, clubs, saloons, and every type of worldly hangout that exists.

Galatians 1:10 challenges our desire to please other men, but I did not understand or appropriate this challenge in my own life. The pain within me cried out for the favor of men and silenced the Word of God in my heart.

Now am I trying to win the favor of men, or of God? Do I seek to please men? If I were still seeking popularity with men, I should not be a bond servant of Christ (the Messiah) (Galatians 1:10 AMP).

Romans 12:2 gives clear direction and a solution that is meant to keep us from the dangers of this world. However, my need to be loved and accepted by others cried louder than the Word of God in my heart. Yes, I wanted the perfect will of God in my life, but I also wanted the ache in my heart to go away. Instead of turning to God for the solution, I turned away from Him.

Do not be conformed to this world (this age), [fashioned after and adapted to its external, superficial customs], but be transformed (changed) by the [entire] renewal of your mind [by its new ideals and its new attitude], so that you may prove [for yourselves] what is the good and acceptable and perfect will of God, even the thing which is good and acceptable and perfect [in his sight for you] (Romans 12:2 AMP).

Although I had given up drinking alcohol and abusing my body, I pretended that I enjoyed the New Orleans jazz clubs and bars because I did not want to be left out. I started to drink again even though I knew my actions did not please God. He had transformed me into a beautiful butterfly and there I was—trying to be a caterpillar again—creeping around as though I did not have wings. However, knowing what God wants does not guarantee that Christians will always do what God wants.

Although I had confessed Jesus as my Savior, I had not accepted His promises or grown in my knowledge of Him. He had not become personal to me. I did not understand that salvation is an on-going work of the Holy Spirit and that I still needed to be healed of many wounds and deep emotional hurts. In fact, I did my best to bury them with Stu and forget the pain of going on without him. I refused to face the woman inside of me that still cried out to be held and comforted.

As a result of those neglected sensual desires, I was a vulnerable babe in Christ and satan knew that all too well. However, I did not know that the enemy took advantage of babies. My instability and weaknesses were a result of self-knowledge instead of God-knowledge. Sadly, my failure to grow in the knowledge and wisdom of God proved to be a grave mistake.

One night in New Orleans I drank too much and fell into a pit of sin. I needed desperately to be comforted and loved as a woman. So, I drank myself into oblivion until I reached a point of no return.

The next morning I woke up in disbelief. *How? How could I possibly have fallen so far in such a short time?* My pounding headache was nothing in comparison to the pain tearing through my heart. Tears poured from my eyes as the previous evening replayed itself in my mind's eye. I tried to turn it off, make it go away, turn back the clock, but it just kept playing one ugly scene after another. I despised myself. The shame was almost too much to bear, but it confronted me every time I looked into the mirror. From somewhere, deep inside of me, a prayer pushed its way up through the heavy lump in my throat, "Oh God...oh God...I'm sorry... how did this happen...oh God, I'm sorry!" I felt like I was dying, but one small part of me struggled to cry out for life, for mercy, and for God's forgiveness.

New Orleans is often called the "City of Sin." After my experience there, my entire salvation was shaken, and that city's name became a reality to me. The enemy had plotted, planned, and waited for the perfect opportunity to offer me a gold-plated temptation so that he could take away the Word, which had been sown in my heart, and cause me to doubt my salvation.

Sinful Behavior Leads to Spiritual Death

Entangled in sin, I started to die spiritually. My joy and peace slipped away day by day. I wanted to cry out for help but I did not know how. My self-esteem and integrity as a Christian gone, I still knew that a Christ-fulfilled life held the answers for me.

I used to tell my testimony to everyone I met. It was such a joy to say "God has saved me through His Son Jesus Christ!" After New Orleans, I could almost feel the enemy laughing at me. "You thought you were so perfect. You thought you were healed. Now look at you, a fine Christian you are!" *How did I get this way?* I wondered. *What happened?*

Let no man say when he is tempted, I am tempted of God: for God cannot be tempted with evil, neither tempteth He any man: But every man is tempted, when he is drawn away of his own lust, and enticed. Then when lust hath conceived, it bringeth forth sin: and sin, when it is finished, bringeth forth death (James 1:13-15).

Not only had I experienced widowhood after Stu's death in a natural sense, but now I faced still another form of widowhood. I found myself with an even greater loss and brokenness in my life. *Did God still love me?* On the brink of uncertainty and fear, I neither respected nor loved myself. How could God possibly love me? The quick-fix and easy answers that I had learned to recite as a new Christian did not work any longer. This superficial knowledge of God was not deep enough to sustain me during the times of temptation and weakness. My wounds, still open from Stu's death, continued to bleed, and I missed him more than ever. I had to face the truth that I was not only a physical widow, but I was a spiritual widow as well.

The Characteristics of a Spiritual Widow

Most people are familiar with the term *widow* as "a woman whose husband has died." God has shown me that people (men and women alike) are *widowed* in many ways. A widow is also someone who is broken as a result of any kind of great loss—the loss of a loved one, the loss of self-esteem, integrity, peace, or perhaps the loss of a right-standing with God. *In essence, the* **widow** *represents a broken state.*

In the traditional sense of *widowhood*, a woman becomes deeply wounded when her husband dies. She often feels as though a part of herself died along with that person because of the love they shared together. Many emotions are experienced during this time, and sometimes we are unsure of our feelings because of the numbness created by this deep wound.

The sorrow that we experience as widows represents a normal progression toward wholeness and healing.

Sorrow is a signal that *something* is missing; an emptiness is present. This sorrow may result from the loss of a loved one or the loss of another part of our lives. This painful grief produces a variety of feelings or emotional responses.

Our feelings are real. They are emotional responses that are triggered by events, circumstances, words, etc. Sometimes these messages are very painful. In my own experience, the pain of losing my husband was accompanied by emotions that eventually led to sinful behavior.

It is imperative that we remain alert and sober-minded, especially during times of emotional distress. We cannot afford to become totally consumed in our sorrow because severe emotional wounds deepen and widen. Then, if those wounds are left untreated, gangrene (sinful behavior) will eventually set in and spread throughout the entire body. (I have addressed the specific needs of traditional *widowhood* in "A Tribute to Traditional Widows" at the end of this book.)

In a broader sense, widowhood also occurs with any sense of loss in our lives. When something or someone is missing, we experience a range of painful emotions. These emotions often result in a loss of self-esteem, personal integrity, a sense of peace, or even our relationship with God.

We may feel unworthy because of something we have done or perhaps something that we perceive as unpardonable. Often we feel as though we will never again be worthy of the love and admiration of others.

The loss of peace can be equated to the lack of a resting place and existing instead in a place of toil and torment. All of us need peace. We are not whole individuals without it. If peace leaves us, we will feel an emptiness in our lives. Anxiety and restlessness will drive us from place to place and produce emotions of fear and insecurity.

A Right Standing With God Is Essential for Life

The loss of a right standing with God is a place of nonfellowship with the Almighty, or the lack of a true awareness of His love, mercy, and grace. Psalm 91 states:

He who dwells in the secret place of the Most High shall remain stable and fixed under the shadow of the Almighty [Whose power no foe can withstand.] ... Because he has set his love upon Me, therefore will I deliver him; **I will set him on high, because he knows and understands My name [has a personal knowledge of My mercy, love, and kindness—trusts and relies on Me, knowing I will never forsake him, no, never]** *(Psalm 91:1,14 AMP).*

When we lose a right standing with God we often feel as though God is no longer with us. In actuality, we are the ones who move away from the secret place of God's presence; but the *feeling* is still one of isolation. When we move away from this place in God, we become prey to the enemy; we waiver back and forth; and our lives become very unstable. We experience the state of *spiritual widowhood* and find ourselves in a downward cycle of emotions, sinful consequences, more emotions, and more sin.

The loss is not the sin. The feeling itself is not the sin. However, the behavior that results from it is either godly or sinful. This behavior will either lead you to God or away from Him.

The emotions of spiritual widowhood, as well as those of traditional widowhood, have the same effect upon us. Each sorrow or loss in our lives has the potential to result in further chaos and turmoil if it is not identified, confronted, and healed.

Selah

Be honest with yourself. Does your life exemplify any of the characteristics noted above? Have you found yourself without a true sense of direction or focus in life because of a loss in your life or brokenness? If so, you can be described as a *spiritual widow.*

Now imagine yourself driving a car into a land of despair. You now have to make a choice. You can continue to drive further into despair, or you can stop and park until you determine how to find hope.

You, too, must learn to identify your feelings and the wounds that they have created or are presently creating. You must identify and confront the reality of your feelings. If emotional wounds have resulted in sinful behavior, you must confess the sin in order to be healed and forgiven.

If we confess our sins, He is faithful and just to forgive us our sins, and to cleanse us from all unrighteousness (1 John 1:9).

Confess your faults one to another, and pray for one another, that ye may be healed. The effectual fervent prayer of a righteous man availeth much (James 5:16).

Chapter 3

Defining the Pain and Naming Our Enemies

Are you a widow or even a spiritual widow? Do you have emotions within you that sometimes conflict with your Christian testimony? Do you wrestle with inner shadows and undefined enemies?

If so, it is time for you to begin to identify the losses, pain, emotions, and sinful consequences in your own life. I recommend that you read this part of the book very slowly, ponder your true feelings, and learn to freely express those hidden emotions. Keep a notebook and actually write down your feelings as you read this chapter. Putting your pain into words is a part of the healing process. Too often we suffer from shadows (the unidentified). Giving your pain a name and identity will help you to put substance to the shadows.

Remember, feelings are only emotional responses. God has created us with emotions. The emotion itself is not sinful. What we do with the emotion sometimes becomes sinful, but for the moment we simply need to identify the feelings themselves and the emotional loss that they stem from.

What Is Pain?

When we speak of pain or healing from pain, we often think of physical pain. What is pain? Pain can be defined as anguish, sorrow, grief, affliction, misfortune, misery, distress, mourning, suffering, or torment, and so on. The *New Lexicon Webster's Dictionary* defines pain as "an unpleasant sensation caused by the stimulation of certain nerves, especially as a result of injury or sickness; a distressing emotion" (Lexicon Publications, Inc., New York, 1988).

God Wants to Heal Our Pain

Isaiah 53:4 states: "Surely He has borne our griefs (sicknesses, weaknesses, and distresses) and carried our sorrows and pain..."(AMP). I believe that our emotional well-being is clearly addressed in these words. Isaiah 53:5 goes on to say that with His stripes we are healed. Therefore, our emotional hurts are as important to God as our physical sicknesses.

Christ died so that our emotions could also be healed. There is no need to turn to unsaved psychiatrists and psychologists for this healing. God has provided the way for you to be whole again.

It is critical for us to be able to define and understand our painful emotions. Our journey through life teaches us that one pain is not really greater than the other. In essence, all hurt must be properly dealt with or the result will be additional hurt. Furthermore, overcoming each hurt builds us into strong, stable human beings who will no longer have a fear of life. Actually, the freedom we gain will cause us to perceive life as an adventure. We will soar and ride on the wings of God's love as we allow Him to make us whole. The prophet Isaiah perfectly describes this freedom in Isaiah 40:30-31.

Even youths grow tired and weary, and young men stumble and fall; but those who hope in the Lord will renew their strength. They will soar on wings like eagles; they will run and not grow weary, they will walk and not be faint (Isaiah 40:30-31 NIV).

It is time to begin. Use your notebook and write down your answers to the following questions. Although your initial answers may be either a simple "yes" or "no," take a few moments to ask yourself *why* you have answered one way or another. Look at the feelings behind your answers and write those down as well. After you have finished writing, go back and underline or circle strong negative emotional words such as fear, anger, emptiness, etc.

The Loss of a Loved One

1. Have you lost someone who was very close to you? Write down his or her name.

2. What did you feel at the time?

3. Did you accept the loss?

4. How long ago did this happen?

5. Are you still able to accept the loss today?

6. Do you still experience emotional responses from this loss? What are they?

7. Do you escape from reality by imagining that your loved one will show up one day and surprise you?

8. Do you sometimes blame that person for leaving you behind?

9. Do you entertain death wishes for yourself?

The Loss of Self-Esteem

1. When you look at yourself in the mirror, do you like what you see? Why or why not?

2. Do you see a beautiful person with potential and purpose in life? Why or why not?

3. Do you see someone whose existence is valuable to the world? Or, do you see someone of little or no value; someone who is unworthy of the love and admiration of others, including God?

4. Have you spent most of your life with a low image of yourself or has low self-image been triggered by a significant loss?

Read the following signs of low self-esteem and note any that you identify with in your notebook. Be aware that these characteristics are not easily identified in ourselves although it is easy to see them in other people. Ask the Holy Spirit to help you see the areas of your life that need healing.

1. The self-righteous individual has difficulty finding any fault in himself or herself, but he is quick to point out the faults and shortcomings of other people. Self-righteous people often try to compensate for their own inadequacies (which they cannot admit) by finding fault with others.

2. A person who is "braggadocious" has a deep need to boast about himself or herself in an effort to boost self-esteem. In other words, "I will tell you how good I am and perhaps I will begin to believe it myself."

3. Someone who tries to buy the affection or recognition of others with gifts and material things is compensating for a deep sense of unworthiness. He feels unloved and unable to be loved for who he is.

4. A person who is immobilized and who refuses to move ahead is often suffering from a sense of low self-esteem. A fear of failure convinces him that he cannot do what needs to be done.

5. People who are insecure suffer from low self-esteem. They do not have confidence in who they are or in their God-given abilities.

6. Individuals with low self-esteem often exhibit instability, a lack of conviction, and an inability to commit themselves to projects that need to be done.

The Loss of Integrity

1. Do you believe that you are morally sound, whole, and complete?

2. Do you feel trustworthy?

3. Do your actions follow your words?

4. How high is your standard of life and what standard is it based on?

5. Is it based on God's Word, current trends in society, or the approval of family and friends?

The Loss of Peace

1. Are you burdened today?

2. Are you burdened on most days?

3. Are you easily frustrated with life?

4. Do you fear life?

5. Are you fearful of making simple decisions?

6. Do you sometimes feel as though you have no resting place?

7. Are you able to identify the source of your peace? What is it?

The Loss of a Right Standing With God

1. Do you truly know your Creator?

2. Have you accepted Jesus Christ as Savior?

3. Do you know Him well enough to trust Him even when things go wrong?

4. Do you have a sin that so easily entangles you?

5. When you fall to this sin, do you feel as though God is far from you or that God hates you?

6. Do you sense God's love, mercy, and grace continuously in your life?

Write a letter to God in your notebook and tell Him how you feel about your relationship with Him. After you finish, go back and read it. Does it sound like you have written it to a stranger, to a friend, or to a close family member?

Other Areas of Loss, Pain, and Brokenness in Your Life

Identify other areas of your life that need healing. Note the time that you believe the pain began. What are the reoccurring symptoms that you experience?

After you have underlined or circled the strong negative words in your answers to the questions of this chapter, review them. Do you see any common enemies that have reappeared from time to time (anger, fear, loneliness, etc.)?

Selah

Expressing our feelings in words helps us to see exactly what we have to deal with in our life. Hopefully, you have taken this matter very seriously and have done this. Remember, you are not alone. There is a God who cares and who wants to help. God's desire is for you to come to Him as a child, admitting that you cannot make it through life on your own. Failure to approach God with honesty will always lead to destruction.

For example, I failed to confront my deep-rooted pain; I fell into sin; and my course in life took on a pattern of self-destruction. You have the opportunity today, right now, to change the course of your life. Confrontation can be a powerful weapon for you.

You can name the pain (your enemy) and confront it before it becomes a sinful behavior. Pain often masks itself in compulsive forms of behavior. For example, pain may be hidden in compulsive spending habits, eating, or lying behaviors. These types of behaviors are often overlooked as sin. Therefore, it is imperative that you adequately name your enemies and confront them before they take hold of your life.

Chapter 4

Running to the Roar

After the pain is identified, it can be confronted. In fact it must be confronted. Like a disease, pain that is not treated always results in some form of death. Our pain actually "roars" within us. Too often, we run from it and try to hide, praying that it will go away. However, the "roar" grows louder with each passing day, like a hungry lion waiting to devour us.

My pain grew louder day by day. When I tried to appease it with the love and approval of others, it only grew worse. Sometimes I tried to hide behind a busy schedule and flurry of activities, but it was always waiting for me when I closed the door at night. At other times I set my mind and heart to ignore it, but regardless of my concentrated effort, it refused to leave. I tried to cover it up with just the right make-up and new hairstyles, but these were only temporary masks. Despite all my efforts, the pain entrenched itself in my heart deeper than ever.

Confrontation Is the Answer

Confronting our pain simply means "to be honest with ourselves and with God about it." We no longer deny the truth or attempt to cover it up with self-righteous Christian actions that only look good on the outside. We stand ready to face it with the Word of God. We *run to the "roar."*

I was neither temperate, balanced, or honest with myself about my emotional state and wounded heart. I did not see myself as a Christian woman who stood in need of God's grace and healing. Therefore, at the height of my Christian zeal, I became self-righteous and allowed my sensual desires to overcome my spiritual dedication to God. Just like Paul said in First Timothy 5:11:

> *As for younger widows, do not put them on such a list. For when their sensual desires overcome their dedication to Christ, they want to marry. Thus they bring judgment on themselves, because they have broken their first pledge. Besides, they get into the habit of being idle and going about from house to house. And not only do they become idlers, but also gossips and busybodies, saying things they ought not to* (1 Timothy 5:11-13 NIV).

How did this happen to me? Why did this happen to me? Yes, I loved God, and I knew He loved me. Yet I could not come to grips with the conflicting feelings deep down inside. Because of my wounded heart, I still operated in the flesh. I did not confront my pain.

Therefore, I sinned, lost right-standing with God, and I also began to hate myself.

I wrote this poem to express how I felt while I struggled with my pain. I had sinned but could not comprehend why. I did know what God had done for me, and I knew that I desperately needed to hold on to that. Jesus was the knot that I held on to.

Life After

I once was at the end of my rope and was slipping off fast. Somehow I managed to tie a knot, a great big knot, and I held on.

I rested at that knot for a while until I gained enough strength to climb back up. This upward climb, however, is so risky and so hard. I have to be careful and take it one step at a time. Many people are cheering me on. Some of them are shouting: "You can do it!"; "Faster!"; "Don't worry, I'll catch you if you fall!"

I know that I could make it and that I could probably climb faster. But, I do know that one wrong move could end my precious life. Furthermore, my upward climb would not have been possible if that knot wasn't established at the end.

I am truly grateful to that mighty knot. I looked up and I said to those people cheering me on: "Where were you when I was falling? The knot is tied. Don't rush me, Don't rush me. All I am asking is that you stay at the top and keep cheering me on. I'll get there, but please let it be in my own time."

The Decision Is Ours

Truthfully, I was the only one who knew what I felt inside and; therefore, I was the only one who could confront those feelings. You are the only one who can confront your feelings. No one else can do it for you. When you are experiencing emotional hurts, many people may offer advice, but you are the only one who knows the depth of the pain that you feel. Therefore, you are the only one that can force yourself to "run to the roar" and be healed. You and I are the ones who make the decision to live by the Spirit of God.

No one can do this for us, not even God. We have to accept our own responsibility to live by the Spirit and not according to the flesh. Healing is a process of putting off the old and putting on the new, accepting God's ways and saying "no" to the ways of the world. Too often, wounded people want others to make their pain go away, make them feel better, or change their life. However, accepting the personal responsibility to live by the Spirit is essential. It is a mark of healing as well as Christian maturity.

...Live by the Spirit, and you will not gratify the desires of the sinful nature. For the sinful nature desires what is contrary to the Spirit, and the Spirit what is contrary to the sinful nature. They are in conflict with each other, so that you do not do what you want....

The acts of the sinful nature are obvious: sexual immorality, impurity and debauchery; idolatry and witchcraft; hatred, discord, jealousy...But the fruit of the Spirit is love, joy, peace, patience, kindness, goodness, faithfulness, gentleness, and self-control...Those who belong to Christ Jesus have crucified the sinful nature with its passions and desires. Since we live by the spirit, let us keep in step with the Spirit (Galatians 5:16-17,19-25 NIV).

We Are not in Debt to the Flesh

*...We are debtors, not to the flesh, to live after the flesh. For if ye live after the flesh, ye shall die: but if ye through the Spirit do mortify the deeds of the body, **ye shall live. For as many as are led by the Spirit of God, they are the sons of God.** For ye have not received the spirit of bondage again to fear; but ye have received the Spirit of adoption, whereby we cry, Abba, Father. The Spirit itself beareth witness with our spirit, that we are the children of God* (Romans 8:12-16).

I am convinced that God does not want us to turn away from our first pledge to live our life for Him. He does not want His Word in our hearts to be like the seed that fell by the wayside, where the Word is sown, where when we have heard it, satan comes immediately to take away the Word that was sown in our hearts. No, God wants His seed to be sown on good soil, so that we will hear the Word, accept it, and bring forth fruit, some 30, 60, or even 100 times what was sown. (See Matthew 13:18-24.)

When we are driven by the flesh, it often indicates that some kind of infirmity exists within us. Infirmity that is not treated or confronted always results in some form of death. My failure to be healed from my initial hurt brought about other reactions in my life that ultimately led to sin.

Shall We Go On Sinning?

Although we were born in sin, God loved us so much that He gave His own life (of flesh) for us. In Romans 6:1-2, Paul stated that believers are dead to sin and alive in Christ. He addressed this question to men who had infirmities in their flesh; men who were not yet healed. "…Shall we go on sinning so that grace may increase?" (NIV) Paul answers, "By no means! We died to sin; how can we live in it any longer?" (NIV)

If we believe in Jesus Christ then we are free, not by our own self-will, but by the grace of God. God blesses us with His grace and mercy. Through this, we receive the greatest blessing of all, *eternal life.* As time goes on, however, we often overlook the fact that we need to humble ourselves in God's blessing. Our lack of humility causes us to establish our own laws and rules. We quickly forget that the atonement was between God and man instead of man and himself. So, we sometimes use God's name and grace as a license to sin.

If we deliberately keep on sinning after we have received the knowledge of the truth, **no sacrifice for sins is left,** *but only a fearful expectation of judgment and of raging fire that will consume the enemies of God.*

Anyone who rejected the law of Moses died without mercy on the testimony of two or three witnesses. How much more severely do you think a man deserves to be punished who has trampled the Son of God under foot, who has treated as an unholy thing the blood of the covenant that sanctified him, and who has insulted the Spirit of grace? ... "And if he shrinks back, I [God] will not be pleased with him." But we are not of those who shrink back and are destroyed, but of those who believe and are saved (Hebrews 10:26-29,38b-39 NIV).

We Have an Enemy

To "not shrink back" is to face the pain and the infirmity that lies within us. To "not shrink back" is to face the enemy.

Be well balanced (temperate, sober of mind), be vigilant and cautious at all times; for that enemy of yours, the devil, roams around like a lion roaring [in fierce hunger], seeking someone to seize upon and devour (1 Peter 5:8 AMP).

If we do not remain alert and cautious we may be devoured by the enemy who roams around like a roaring lion. This is true at all times and especially during times of pain. It is imperative that we run to the roar of the lion (our pain) and confront it once and for all so that we may be healed.

Run to the Roar

My pastor once preached a story about the law of the jungle practiced by the lion family. This story adds further clarity to the process of confronting our pain.

When lions become old they can no longer go out and seize their prey for food. There is an unwritten law between the younger and older lions. The older lion will station himself behind a bush, completely out of sight of the alleged prey; and the younger lion will position himself just a few feet away. At the sight of the prey, the older lion will bellow out the loudest roar he can come up with. It is almost inevitable that at the sound of the great roar, the prey will flee terrified in the opposite direction, only to run straight into the younger lions. Then all of the lions dine sufficiently. The only way to assure safety in that kind of situation is to *run to the roar.*

Therefore, whenever there are unresolved issues in your life, do not run *from* them, run *to* them. When you run away from the issues of life, such as your pain and your dishonesty with yourself about yourself; you will always run to destruction. But if you *run to the roar*, you will find that there is nothing to fear.

Selah

Hopefully, you have readied yourself to confront your pain and its sinful consequences. You are prepared to honestly face the pain in your life because you do not want to continue to gratify the desires of your flesh, and you do not want to go on willfully sinning. If you have, you have taken a major step on your road to recovery. If not, take a few moments to consider the consequences if you refuse to take this step.

Running to the roar does not mean that you are responsible for your healing. It does mean that you come to a place that you are willing to cooperate with God in the process of your healing.

When Christ died for us, all of our sins were instantly forgiven. His stripes healed us. From God's perspective, this is a finished work. However, this has to become a reality for us. We must see ourselves, our pain, and our sin on the cross with Him.

This confession of faith needs a meaningful expression so that you will be able to look back and say "It is finished. This is on the cross of Jesus." Praying about it with another Christian is preferable, but if you do not have someone that you feel secure with, I suggest that you write out your prayer in your notebook. You may want to draw a large cross on one page. Write the name of Jesus at the top of the cross and then put your own name underneath. Write your enemies (pain and sin) on the cross as well.

Chapter 5

Humbling Ourselves

The only way to break the self-destructive pattern of pain is through humility. The confrontation of pain in our lives is a humbling experience. Most of the time we do not welcome the conviction of the Holy Spirit when He puts His finger on a specific area in our life that needs healing.

In my own experience, I knew that the sin was wrong, but this sin still became my god. I pushed the conviction of the Holy Spirit aside because I was satisfied with my own righteousness and my superficial level of faith. Self-righteousness always justifies (makes excuses for) our sinful behaviors.

Oh, how wrong I was. I will never forget the day that I fell to my knees and repented for my wicked ways. I realized that I was just a sinner cleansed, and washed by the blood of Jesus. *Oh, how precious is the flow that made me white as snow, there is nothing like the blood of Jesus.*

Although I had confessed Jesus as my Savior many months before, I had failed to make Him personal in my life. I had not experienced and grown in a knowledge of His love, grace, mercy, and peace. I had not heeded the conviction of the Holy Spirit. That day, on my knees, I humbled myself before God. I acknowledged my sin and immersed myself in His mercy and grace.

I had allowed my sensual desires, the ones Paul wrote about in Ephesians 2:3, to dominate my life. Instead of resting in Christ's sufficiency, I made many mistakes trying to find love outside of what God had given me. I had grown anxious for a mate and just wanted to get married. I was actually running my own life instead of waiting for the Lord. I had brought my old prideful nature into my new life, and my self-righteousness opened the door for a spirit of bondage to creep in. But, Proverbs 16:18 says "Pride goeth before destruction [or a fall]." And yes, I fell. But, the Lord picked me up and continued to heal me!

Jesus Is the Only Way

Jesus is truly the only Way, the Truth, and the Life. Young widows, listen, I am speaking to you if you have ears to hear. Our hurt stirs up all types of emotions, including our sensual desires. But you have a choice. Choose life and peace, not as the world gives but as Christ gives.

Christians, listen, I am speaking to you if you have ears to hear. Salvation does not insulate us from the temptations of the enemy. If you have been *widowed* through a loss or deep brokenness in your life, you are vulnerable to the wiles of satan. He will use your loss, your pain, and your emotions to deceive you and convince you that the way of sin is the way of peace and happiness.

I fell into the sins of idolatry (worshiping other people and things instead of God) and lust. Yours may be something else. You may have a love of money or an obsessive desire for fine material things. You may be holding a deep resentment against someone, or you may be unwilling to let go of a painful memory. Alcohol and drug addiction may eat at you. You may be dishonest in business matters and untrustworthy in friendships. Perhaps you are abusive to a member of your family. Many people have a need to control and manipulate others. There may be idols in your life that are elevated above God. The list goes on and on. These sins only produce more pain and disappointment. They continue to wound us and destroy our relationship with God. Yes, even upstanding Christians face these battles on a daily basis!

Humility Heals

Facing our sinfulness with a humble heart is part of the healing process. *If humility is the fear of the Lord, which is the beginning of wisdom, then when we are humbled, we begin a process of building stability and strength of character* (see Prov. 9:10). Without this true wisdom of God, we remain unstable and weak in our salvation.

Isaiah 33:6 says: "And wisdom and knowledge shall be the stability of thy times, and strength of salvation: the fear of the Lord is his treasure." It is imperative that we humble ourselves before the Almighty God and wait for Him to exalt us. We cannot submit to our anxious and prideful hearts; they will lead us into temptation.

Pride Always Opposes God

We must always keep in remembrance that pride was the downfall of lucifer. Isaiah 14:12-14 briefly describes the events surrounding satan's fall.

How art thou fallen from heaven, O Lucifer, son of the morning! how art thou cut down to the ground, which didst weaken the nations! For thou has said in thine heart, I will ascend into heaven, I will exalt my throne above the stars of God: I will sit also upon the mount of the congregation, in the sides of the north: I will ascend above the height of the clouds; I will be like the most High (Isaiah 14:12-14).

Satan was so prideful that he convinced one-third of the angels that he was more powerful than God. Although God could have destroyed satan, he did not because He wanted satan to fear (respect) Him instead. If we develop the type of pride that satan has, we too will experience the wrath of God. Why experience God's wrath when we can have His love? We must, however, choose to love God. But, loving God requires a reverence of Him and a respect for Him drawn by our own love.

Lessons in Humility

Humility must be learned. It cannot be taught because pride cannot receive instruction. Humility is only learned when one is made low and *pride always goes before a fall* (see Prov. 16:18).

I believe that man is first broken (humbled) so that he might acknowledge and accept God as his Creator, Savior, and Lord. After man accepts this knowledge, he must also be broken and tried in order for the character of God to be reproduced in Him. He must remain pliable so that he will come forth as pure "gold."

The Bible proves this point in the book of Job. Job 23:10 says, "But He knows the way that I take; when He has tested me, I will come forth as gold" (NIV).

God is putting Christians through lessons of humility in order to produce that Christ-like quality in us. He has a hope and a future for each individual. The enemy wants to destroy our future, but when pride falls the power of the enemy also falls. We need to be sensitive to those areas in our lives that are susceptible to pride and commit them to the Lord on a daily basis.

Humility is often a misunderstood word because, from a secular perspective, the experience of being humbled before men is often embarrassing. It destroys our self-esteem and does little to enhance our lives. Men exalt themselves at the expense of one another.

Humility before God, however, can be a beautiful and cleansing experience. We bow down and He lifts us up. We deny ourselves and accept Him. We place our human strength under God's control. Consequently, our humility before God causes us to do all things in lowliness of mind instead of out of selfish ambition and vain conceit (see Phil. 2:3 NIV). As a result, God rewards us with a life filled with His abundant grace—a life that rewards us with favor, good understanding, and high esteem in the sight of God and man (Proverbs 3:4 AMP).

Sister Celeste, an evangelist, once defined humility in one of her sermons:

"The fear of the Lord— (beginning of wisdom):
 The denying of self and all of its desires.
 To respect God.
 To reverence God.
 To have an attitude of obedience drawn by
  love.
 Not falling into the sin that so easily entangles
  you; because you don't want to hurt God.
  (This is the essence of love being demon-
   strated.)
The rewards of humility found in Proverbs 22:4
are:
 The fear of the Lord, riches, honor, and life.
 Prosperity (blessings in due season)."

Selah

Have you named your enemy (your pain, its emotional imbalance, and perhaps sinful behavior)? Have you "run to the roar" and confronted your enemy with the truth? If so, it is time to humble yourself before God and face Him with humility and a total surrender.

It is time to immerse yourself in God's mercy, receive His grace, and allow Him to touch those areas in your life that need the conviction of His Holy Spirit. Remember Isaiah 33:6 (NIV) says that the fear of the Lord is the "key" to these treasures. Pride must go and the fear of the Lord must come.

Chapter 6

The New Birth

Perhaps you are like I was, putting off a Christian commitment and church attendance until a convenient time in the future. Or, perhaps you already attend a church and consider yourself a Christian. Receiving Jesus Christ as Savior is more than a decision to attend church or to become involved in religious activities. It is a commitment of faith that says, "I am willing to receive the love and forgiveness that Jesus is extending to me. I am willing to embrace the Son of God and to allow Him to become a part of my life."

If you have not accepted Jesus Christ as your personal Savior, I want to urge you to begin thinking about that possibility right now. I am not asking you to join a church or subscribe to a religious philosophy. I am asking you to accept the gift of eternal salvation that is yours for the asking. It is a free gift. You cannot do anything to earn it or to be worthy enough to receive it. Jesus has done everything that needs to be done. He has paid the price for your life. The debt for your sins has been paid.

Just as Christ knew in His heart that He had to do the will of the Father, we have to know in our hearts that God sent Jesus Christ to this earth to die for us. The question of salvation must be settled. This is the place that the new birth begins to have its full effect in our lives. We receive the promise of eternal salvation as well as healing for our lives today.

For God so loved the world, that He gave His only begotten Son, that whosoever believeth in Him should not perish, but have everlasting life (John 3:16).

But He was wounded for our transgressions, He was bruised for our guilt and iniquities; the chastisement [needful to obtain] peace and well-being for us was upon Him, and with the stripes [that wounded Him] we are healed and made whole (Isaiah 53:5 AMP).

That if thou shalt confess with thy mouth the Lord Jesus, and shalt believe in thine heart that God hath raised Him from the dead, thou shalt be saved. For with the heart man believeth unto righteousness; and with the mouth confession is made unto salvation (Romans 10:9-10).

For ye have not received the spirit of bondage again to fear; but ye have received the Spirit of adoption, whereby we cry, Abba, Father. The Spirit itself beareth witness with our spirit, that we are the children of God (Romans 8:15-16).

Right now, some of you may be wondering how to receive the Spirit of adoption. The first step is to ask Jesus into your heart. It is not a complicated process. It does not require religious understanding or classes in theology. The only thing you need to have is a desire to know Jesus as your personal Savior, Healer, and Friend. In time, He will become much more to you, but this is a good place to begin. You can do this by repeating this prayer:

"Father, I love you. Thank you for caring enough for me to heal me and make me whole. I acknowledge the fact that Your Son Jesus Christ is Lord and that You raised Him from the dead so that I could be saved, healed, and made whole. I accept Jesus into my life as my personal Lord and Savior. I accept Your will for me to be healed, and I thank You for it. Amen."

Some of you have already prayed this prayer and you consider yourselves Christians, but you have not found the peace that is part of God's Kingdom. You need to accept the Father's will for you to be healed. You need to be able to accept the power, love, and sound mind that God has already given to you. "For God hath not given us the spirit of fear; but of power, and of love, and of a sound mind" (2 Tim. 1:7).

Let the healing process work out patience, and let patience work out the healing process. They work hand in hand. Patience is one of the keys to a successful healing and healing is a process. Jesus experienced *birth, death, burial, and resurrection.* We must also go through these phases before we experience total rest and healing.

1. You began the *birth* phase when you prayed the previous prayer. (For those of you who may have disregarded the prayer, there are no shortcuts to wholeness. I tried many other ways to reach wholeness, but found it only through a personal relationship with my Lord and Savior Jesus Christ.)

2. You must *die* to your old life. This may sound difficult, but it is a basic principle of life. Yesterday is gone. Tomorrow lies before you, and you are alive today. You must be willing to let go of yesterday's pain.

3. Your old life is *buried* in Christ. This means that we refuse to allow the pain from yesterday to rule over us today. When we submit ourselves (our mind, will, and emotions) to God, God's Spirit reigns in love, peace, and joy.

4. Finally, you must let the Spirit of the Living God *resurrect* you. Allow God to give you a new life of hope and healing. Let go of the past pain and receive today's blessings. Come out of your tomb of despair and hopelessness. Allow the Son (Jesus Christ) to shine in your life.

Isaiah 40:30-31 gives a beautiful picture of this resurrection life. Pain makes us weary. It saps the strength from our lives and exhausts our sense of pleasure.

However, the Lord wants to renew our strength and give us hope.

Even youths grow tired and weary, and young men stumble and fall; but those who hope in the Lord will renew their strength. They will soar on wings like eagles; they will run and not grow weary, they will walk and not be faint (Isaiah 40:30-31 NIV).

Those who hope in the Lord shall renew their strength. It is possible for you to mount up on God's love, flap those wings, and fly like an eagle! You now belong to the Father! You are free through the hope you have placed in Him. A personal relationship with the Father through our Lord Jesus Christ gives us the strength to go on even though we might feel weak and helpless. I once heard a song that literally sums up my testimony during one phase of my widowhood.

Lately I've been winning battles left and right, but even winners can get wounded in the fight.
People say that I'm amazing strong beyond my years.
But, they don't see inside of me I am hiding all my tears.
They don't know that I go running home when I fall down.
They don't know who picks me up when no one is around.
I drop my sword and cry for just awhile.
Deep inside this armor THE WARRIOR IS A CHILD.

Unafraid because his armor is the best.
But, even soldiers need a quiet place to rest.
People say that I'm amazing, never face retreat.
But, they don't see the enemies that lay me at his feet.
They don't know that I go running home when I fall down.
They don't know who picks me up when no one is around.
I dropped my sword and looked up for a smile.
Deep inside this armor THE WARRIOR IS A CHILD.[1]

Although my decision to accept Jesus Christ gave me a new hope, I did not immediately understand what it meant to cast my burdens on Jesus or to make Him Lord of my life. When I accepted Christ, I thought that I would immediately transform into a whole person with no more cares. *What a relief*, I thought, *my cares are all gone*. I did not realize that accepting Christ was only the first step and that I had to put forth some effort to grow in the knowledge of Christ, which would then lead to the manifestation of God's healing virtues. Proverbs 9:10 says, "...the knowledge of the Holy One is insight and understanding" (AMP).

You may not understand what it means to *let go* of the past, to *die* to the old life, to be *buried* in Christ, or

---

1.   *The Warrior Is A Child* by Twila Paris. Copyright © 1984. Used by permission.

to be *resurrected* by the Living God. Do not be discouraged. The Lord knows exactly what you need to learn and how. As long as you are willing to put forth the effort to grow in a knowledge of Christ, He will teach you everything you need to know.

Selah

I pray that you have taken this first step with Jesus. Many of you will identify with the joys that I have discovered and the mistakes that I have made on the path of healing. Others may be taking these steps for the first time. Regardless of where you are at on your personal journey to wholeness, remember, *you are not alone.* If you feel alone, you only need to whisper His name in prayer.

"Jesus, I need Your strength. Right now I feel [describe exactly how you feel]. *You are always here, ready to help me when I need help. Please fill me with Your love right now. Restore to me the joy of my salvation and hold me up with Your Spirit. Thank you for saving me and for healing me. I do want to grow in the knowledge of Christ. Thank You for the plan that You have for my life. Amen."*

Chapter 7

Jehovah Rophe—
Our Healer

When we humble ourselves before God, His Holy Spirit restores to us the joy of our salvation (see Ps. 51:12). A repentant heart restores our fellowship with God. Once again we are able to delight in the personal intimacy that God wants to have with each one of us. We are eager to press on to those things of maturity that will keep us in the hour of temptation and be our strong deliverer in the hour of trial. No longer satisfied with a weak, superficial faith, we want to grow up in Christ Jesus.

Till we all come in the unity of the faith, and of the knowledge of the Son of God, unto a perfect man, unto the measure of the stature of the fulness of Christ (Ephesians 4:13).

Jesus Is Lord

This means that we begin to know Jesus not only as Savior, but also as Lord, Healer, and all that He is. The stripes on His back have healed us so we acknowledge Him as Jehovah Rophe (our Healer). He is Jehovah Jireh (our Provider), and Jehovah Nissi (our Banner). When we acknowledge Him as Lord, we give Him permission to reign over all areas of our lives. If we let Him reign over every area, then we allow Him to be everything that we need Him to be and all that He is. We settle in our hearts that Jesus is the Prince of peace, Lord of lords, and King of kings.

We must see Him as the Author and Finisher of our faith. Also, we need to know that He is the Lily of the Valley, the Bright and Morning Star. God is our Father. He clothes the birds and the flowers, and He knows the number of hairs on our head.

These Things Must Be Settled

God Wants to Heal You

First, you and I must settle in our hearts that the Father truly loves us and that He wants to heal us physically, emotionally, and spiritually. He does not want us to feel good today and bad tomorrow. Our hearts should be at peace. We are not created to carry the pain and burdens that sometimes overwhelm our lives.

He is Jehovah Rophe, the God that heals us. Jesus did not heal people because they were perfect people or always full of faith. He did not heal them because they prayed the right way and did the right things. He healed them because He loved them and He had compassion on them. God loves you today. He has more compassion for you than any man could possibly have.

God's Word clearly states that He wants us healed from both the physical and emotional hurts of this life. Isaiah 53:4 states: "Surely He has borne our griefs (sicknesses, weaknesses, and distresses) and carried our sorrows and pains..." (AMP). I believe that our emotional well-being is clearly addressed in these words. Isaiah 53:5 goes on to say that with His stripes we are healed. Therefore, our emotional hurts are equally as important to God as our physical sicknesses. Individuals often turn to unsaved psychiatrists and psychologists for healing from emotional hurts, but Christ died so that our emotions could be healed as well.

Do You Want to Be Healed?

Second, we must want to be healed. God wants to heal us, but some people simply do not want to be healed. They have learned to depend upon their pain (physical, emotional, and spiritual). Pain often illicits a measure of extra attention and sympathy from other people. Relationships become ingrained with co-dependency. One person needs to be needed in a painful situation. Another one uses the pain to keep the relationship intact. There are many reasons why a person may not want to be healed, but not one of them agrees with the Word of God. God wants for you and I to live a life of wholeness. He needs a people who are whole, healed, and ready to minister in His name.

The Word of God

Third, the Word of God must be settled. As we make God real in our lives by studying who He is, we must also remember that He provided us with a book of promises. For example, First Corinthians 12:9 describes "healing" as a gift. So, let us take advantage of all of God's precious promises.

The Bible might have been a dusty book at one time, but when God becomes real to us, this book becomes a collection of love letters penned by the Holy Spirit. Every word has been written just for us. The words seem to *live*, and we begin to hear the voice of our trusted Friend and Counselor.

When we read our Bibles, we should be able to hear God speak to us about the areas of our lives that need healing. As we read about the victorious life of the Christian, our hearts should leap with joy because we know that these promises are for us. We can be whole. We can be healed. We can confront the pain in our lives.

We need to know and believe what the Word of God says. It must be a strong weapon in our hands, ready to silence the enemy (see Heb. 4:12; Eph. 6:17). We have to step beyond comfortable Christianity that allows us to keep our sins hidden and out of sight. Sin must become an enemy to us, and the Word of God must become our Sword. Our conduct and rule for life must be found within the pages of Scripture, not on the lips of friends or on city streets.

It is impossible to stand and confront the pain in our life without the Word of God. Our flesh gives in and submits to pain. The Word of God, however, never submits to pain. We need to have the Word of God in our hearts and on our lips.

Of course we will all go through Gethsemanes. There will be times that we want to give up, and our hearts will tremble with fear. Nonetheless, the Father's healing hand is always with us. Only the Great Physician can perform a successful operation on our soul. Let the healing process begin by allowing the God of peace to crush your enemy. Use Romans 16:20 as a weapon to stomp the enemy. "And the God of peace shall bruise Satan under your feet shortly...." Fearlessly brace yourself to the enemy and boldly confront it with the authority given to you in the Word of God.

We Are Powerless Without Him

Fourth and finally, it must be settled that we are totally powerless without Him. As we endure in this life we must constantly run to His feet or learn to stay at His feet for renewal and strength because He is a defender of widows as stated in Psalm 68:5. God's Word shows us all the things that He is to us. My healing increased as I studied and accepted who God is.

God's Word Says That He is:

Jesus	Matthew 1:21
Wonderful Counselor	Isaiah 9:6
Mighty God	Isaiah 9:6
Everlasting Father	Isaiah 9:6

Prince of Peace	Isaiah 9:6
Lamb of God	John 1:29
Prince of Life	Acts 3:15
Lord God Almighty	Revelation 15:3
King of Saints	Revelation 15:3
Root and Offspring of David	Revelation 22:16
Bright and Morning Star	Revelation 22:16
Word of Life	1 John 1:1
Author and Finisher of our Faith	Hebrews 12:2
Jesus Christ the Righteous	1 John 2:1
The Way, Truth, and Life	John 14:6
Dayspring from on High	Luke 1:78
Lord of All	Acts 10:36
I Am	John 8:58
Son of God	John 1:34
Shepherd and Bishop	1 Peter 2:25
Messiah	John 1:41(NIV)
Chief Cornerstone	Ephesians 2:20
Lord God Omnipotent	Revelation 19:6
Righteous Judge	1 Timothy 4:8
Light of the World	John 8:12
Head (over all things)	Ephesians 1:22
The Lamb	Revelation 22:1
Lord Jesus Christ	Acts 15:11
Chief Shepherd	1 Peter 5:4
The Resurrection and the Life	John 11:25
Horn of Salvation	Luke 1:69
El Shaddai—The breasty one	Genesis 49:25
El Elyon—God over all	Genesis 14:19
Jehovah Rophe—Our healer	Exodus 15:26

Jehovah Nissi—Our banner	Exodus 17:15
Jehovah Shalom—Our peace	Judges 6:23
	Isaiah 9
Jehovah Roi—Shepherd and Pilot	Psalm 23:1
	John 15
Jehovah Jireh—Our provider	Genesis 22:14
Jehovah Tsidkenu—our righteousness	
	2 Corinthians 5:21
Jehovah Shammah—He is always there	Ezekiel 48:35
Alpha and Omega	Revelation 1:8

Surely, He is the God that heals us. The healing process will continue as we bury ourselves in God. (See Exodus 15:26 and Isaiah 30:26.) First seek the Kingdom where the Healer (God) dwells, and wait for Him to bless you with His promise of healing.

Selah

Hebrews 11:6 states that He who draws near to God must first believe that He exists and that He is a rewarder of those who diligently seek Him. After you study who God really is, practice meditating on the nature of God. As you meditate on God's nature, He will reward you with a time of supernatural refreshing.

Chapter 8

Abiding in the Vine

I am the true vine, and My Father is the gardener. He cuts off every branch in Me that bears no fruit, while every branch that does bear fruit He prunes so that it will be even more fruitful. You are already clean because of the word I have spoken to you. Remain in Me, and I will remain in you. No branch can bear fruit by itself; it must remain in the vine. Neither can you bear fruit unless you remain in Me (John 15:1-4 NIV).

Our fruits of healing and wholeness can only be manifested if we remain in the true Vine. Anything grown apart from this true Vine will surely die. When we start to reconnect ourselves to the true Vine, the enemy has a tendency to bring old sinful ways back to our remembrance. However, God's Word also says in Second Corinthians 10:5 that we are to cast down imaginations and "every high thing that exalted itself against the knowledge of God." We are to take those things captive so that they may obey Christ. Our old nature exalts itself against the knowledge of God. We must capture those thoughts and make them obey Christ.

In the early stages of my widowhood, I sought after external fulfillment to satisfy the desire for physical closeness that was deep inside me—a desire that was out of control because I was not whole. I thought that I would be totally healed if I found someone to satisfy my physical needs. *However, I later found out that my healing could never be found in a person; rather, healing is found only in the true Vine.*

The Lord told me that I had to be sure of who my source was. He showed me that He was my only source and that I could do nothing without Him. The physical relationship that I longed for never succeeded because I tried to make it work without acknowledging my source, the true Vine (Jesus).

Our Rightful Place in God

When I finally accepted the fact that Jesus was Lord over me and that God had given me Jesus for victory in this life, as well as for my salvation, I took my rightful place as a child of God. As I began to see myself the way God saw me, I was able to take one more step toward total healing and wholeness. If we expect to be healed, we must let go of ourselves, give God full reign over our lives, and humble ourselves before the Almighty God so that He can lift us up.

I thank the Lord for showing me myself so that I could put *self* to death. After I reached this stage of death, I allowed God to heal me. I needed to cast down all other imaginations and every vain thought that exalted itself against the knowledge of Him (see 2 Cor. 10:5).

This means that I need to say "no" to some of the thoughts that come into my mind. Every time a vain thought or an ungodly imagination rises up in our minds, a decision has to be made. We either go with it or cut it off. Pain breeds thoughts of pity, selfishness, desperation, etc. Lies come forth from pain. I battled with all of these and more, and I had to learn how to make the decision to put these thoughts and lies to death.

No one else could do it for me. If my pain said, "You are unlovable," I needed to say "I refuse to believe this lie; the Father loved me enough to send Jesus. Jesus loved me enough to die for me. The Holy Spirit loves me enough to live in me." Then I was able to develop a personal relationship with the Father. In Him I found the freedom to move forward and be totally healed!

The Baptism in the Holy Spirit

In earlier chapters I shared the fact that after my initial confession of faith, I moved from church to church, searching for the right one. During this time, I met many believers who consistently spoke of the baptism in the Holy Spirit. They described the Holy Spirit as a great power that lived inside of them, and they said that He guided them and gave them power to face life's difficulties.

Although I was curious about the Baptism in the Holy Spirit, I was also somewhat skeptical. I envisioned losing total control and a great power overtaking me.

This thought terrified me, but I saw no evidence of this taking place in the lives of others. As distrustful as I was, my curiosity and desire to know more about God gradually diminished my suspicions.

I received the Baptism in the Holy Spirit one night at a church service after the pastor preached about the importance of utilizing our faith to receive all that God has to offer. He asked everyone who had a desire to be baptized in the Holy Spirit to come forward for prayer.

I remember trying to decide whether or not I wanted this experience. Finally, I made a decision to use my faith as the pastor encouraged us to do. After all, I believed that God loved me and that He would not allow me to receive anything that would hurt me.

That night, some of the elders of the church prayed for me to receive the Baptism. As the elders prayed, I closed my eyes and concentrated on the fact that God wanted me to experience more of Him. While my eyes were closed, I felt an unusual sensation deep down in my belly. The sensation tingled and rumbled, like water flowing through my innermost being. John 7:38-39 states: "He that believeth on Me, as the scripture hath said, out of his belly shall flow rivers of living water. (But this spake He of the Spirit, which they that believe on Him should receive...."

Although I believe I received the Spirit of God the moment that I first believed in Him and received Him as my Savior, this new experience manifested God's

Spirit in my life in a tangible way. This manifestation is recorded throughout the Bible.

> *"I baptize you with water for repentance. But after me will come one who is more powerful than I, whose sandals I am not fit to carry. He will baptize you with the Holy Spirit..."* (Matthew 3:11 NIV).

> *For John baptized with water, but not many days from now you shall be baptized with (placed in, introduced into) the Holy Spirit* (Acts 1:5 AMP).

> *And they were all filled (diffused throughout their souls) with the Holy Spirit...* (Acts 2:4 AMP).

I believe that the Baptism in the Holy Spirit represents the believer's acknowledgment of God's indwelling Spirit. It is a supernatural phenomenon that manifests the fusing of man's spirit with God's Spirit. (Through sin, man's fellowship with God was broken, but God so loved the world that He gave His Son Jesus so that we should not perish; but that we might have eternal life. [See John 3:16.]) Because God's Spirit resides within, there is no need to face life's troubles without God's help.

The Fullness of Joy

God is closer to us than we realize. When we encounter His presence, we experience total fullness of joy. This joy can be described as the type of joy that the world can never give. It is everlasting and comes through our knowledge of God's love for us. We need this joy to strengthen us daily.

When God is personal to us, we learn to trust Him and be joyful even when we hurt. This personal relationship with the Father causes us to acknowledge the fact that God is allowing us to go through all of our trials and tribulations until we are made mature in Him. Our healing is a process that produces patience and endurance if we do not faint. Through all our pain, trials, and difficulties we must learn how to be full of joy.

Moreover [let us also be full of joy now!] let us exult and triumph in our troubles and rejoice in our sufferings, knowing that pressure and affliction and hardship produce patient and unswerving endurance. And endurance (fortitude) develops maturity of character (approved faith and tried integrity). And character [of this sort] produces [the habit of] joyful and confident hope of eternal salvation. Such hope never disappoints or deludes or shames us, for God's love has been poured out in our hearts through the Holy Spirit Who has been given to us. While we were yet in weakness [powerless to help ourselves], at the fitting time Christ died for (in behalf of) the ungodly (Romans 5:3-6 AMP).

Abiding Patience

Before I knew Jesus, I was young, energetic, and to some extent obnoxious. When I came into a saving knowledge of the Lord Jesus Christ, my personality did not automatically change. My walk with the Lord has been a constant purging of the flesh in order for me to attain the state of patience that is necessary for me to fully know God and trust Him. I believe that this purging is necessary for all God's children because even Jesus had to put His own flesh to death.

For example, before Jesus was arrested by the government, He struggled with His will and His Father's will. Patience (trust) allowed Jesus to see and yield to the Father's will when He was in the garden of Gethsemane. I do not think anyone of us can imagine what Jesus had to go through, but patience (trust) caused Him to persevere. The government came and arrested Him. At the time of His arrest, He was at peace with Himself because He had already settled it in His heart and knew that the Father's will had to be done. (See Matthew 26:36-50.)

Jesus Knew the Secret of Abiding

Just as Jesus knew the secret of abiding in His Father, you and I must learn the secret of abiding in Jesus. We do this by daily trusting in His love and relying on Him for everything we need. He gives us grace, peace, joy, contentment, love, and everything else that our hearts might long for. We do not have to listen to the desires of our flesh and fall into sin. He gives us a heart that longs after Him when we diligently seek Him through prayer, worship, and a consistent study of His Word.

It is important to note that each believer must yield daily to the Spirit of God that dwells within. Although He dwells within us, He does not override our will or desires. Therefore, we must give up our will and trust

God to direct our lives daily. A life directed by God's Spirit is incomparable to the life we may try to lead by ourselves.

Selah

Are you abiding in the true Vine today? Do you have a heart that longs after Him? Take a spiritual inventory right now. Peace, joy, love, patience, trust...are they yours? These are essential for the healing process in your life. Begin today to develop a consistent devotional life and spend time developing your relationship with Jesus.

Close your eyes and meditate on who God is. Go back over the names that describe Him (see Chapter 7). With your eyes closed, tell God that you want to know Him in a real way. Write out this prayer request in your notebook. By faith, sense His awesome presence. In God's presence, His liquid love is powerful enough to saturate us and cure us from our pain.

If you have not received the Baptism in the Holy Spirit, I urge you to prayerfully consider this dimension of Christian experience. The manifestation of His Holy Spirit strengthens and empowers the believer's life to abide in God's presence on a daily basis.

"Jesus, your Word promises me that You will baptize me with Your Holy Spirit. I know that You love me and that You want me to live in the fullness of joy. I know that You want me to abide in You every day and yield my life to You. I need Your Spirit to help me and to empower me to live my life in ways that are pleasing to You. Please baptize me with Your Holy Spirit. I receive the love that You are pouring out for me right now, and I believe that Your living waters will flow out of my innermost being. Amen."

Chapter 9

Standing Firm
in His Liberty

After I realized the importance of having a personal
relationship with God and abiding in the Vine, there
were still some days that I felt stronger than others.
But, I knew that the Lord wanted me to stand firm in
His liberty. He wanted me to let go of my capabilities,
wants, desires, and hurts so that He could fill me and
keep me filled. He wanted to be Lord over those attri-
butes 100 percent of the time.

There comes a time when we must make Jesus Lord
over our entire life—even Lord over our unstable emotions. I believe that during the emotional periods of instability, we actually experience self-pity. Although it is
a natural response for us to cry, feel hurt, angry, bitter,
or whatever accompanies our lament, the time will
come when we must *accept the fact that Jesus is with us always.* Even though we have felt forsaken in the past or
let down by our failures and circumstances in life, Jesus

never fails us, nor does He leave or forsake us. He loves us so much. And we can show our love toward Him by making Him supreme—even over our unstable emotions.

This chapter describes a few of the emotional instabilities that I experienced after I was totally humbled in my Christian walk and even after I acknowledged the need to make God personal. However, I thank God for allowing me to experience all the feelings described here because it was through these times that I learned to totally stand firm in the liberty that Christ gave me. Through these events, I learned to exchange my emotional instability for a firm foundation of God's love.

This foundation is like a tree planted by the water that sends out its roots by the stream. It does not fear when heat comes; its leaves are always green. It has no worries in a year of drought and never fails to bear fruit (see Jer. 17:8). I am sharing these experiences with you because I want to encourage you to continue to be *honest* about your pain. God does not want us to pretend to be what we are not. We need to honestly confront our times of instability in order to be healed.

When I Am Weak, I Am Strong

One day, I awoke rejoicing in the Lord's day and felt inordinately spirited, as though I could handle any obstacle in my path. There was a real assurance that God was with me that day, and I felt very strong because I was standing on the Word of God that says He will never leave me nor forsake me (see Heb. 13:5). So, I gave the day my all, and I was definitely on top of the world. I felt as though I had reached another peak in my spiritual journey. I had conquered and was victorious!

As the day ended, however, I began to wonder why I felt so exhausted. My high had become a low. The day turned out to be mentally overbearing. By 4:00 p.m. I was completely drained. I had given my all at work that day and I felt a little weak. This familiar feeling of weakness had often caused me to regress in the past, so I feared it.

First I was really tired, then my emotions crept in, and then I started missing Stu all over again. I thought that, after all this time, I should not be so emotional. I was afraid to be human. In other words, I tried my best not to deal with the loss that still held me in chains. Then suddenly two Scriptures became a reality to me.

Stand fast therefore in the liberty wherewith Christ hath made us free, and be not entangled again with the yoke of bondage (Galatians 5:1).

...I delight in weaknesses, in insults, in hardships, in persecutions, in difficulties. For when I am weak, then I am strong (2 Corinthians 12:10 NIV).

I realized that the way I felt all day was just part of the progressive process of healing. If I never felt this way, I would constantly feel that I was a super-human, able to leap any obstacle in a single bound. Yes, and all by *myself*. It is dangerous when we think that *self* is accomplishing something. We can never be totally healed if *self* is in the way.

Galatians 5:1 states, "...wherewith Christ hath made us free" and Second Corinthians 12:10 says, "For when I am weak, then I am strong" (NIV). Jesus needs a place deep within us where He can dwell. So that whenever we are weak, He becomes our strength.

What is my point? My point is that it is still okay to have strong feelings for our loved ones, even years after they are gone, or to reflect on our past failures or perhaps recurring feelings of inferiority. I believe it is necessary that we admit to these feelings so that we can constantly grow closer to God—the only One who can truly comfort us through His Holy Spirit. I believe that if we totally forget where we came from, we will also forget who has brought us out. There are times when we just have to remind ourselves that there is still a balm in Gilead and a Great Physician willing and able to comfort us. I am not suggesting that we cope or dwell on our pain. I am merely saying that although we may have memories of the events that triggered our pain, standing firm in God's liberty causes the pain to totally lose its sting.

The prophet Jeremiah inquired: "Is there no balm in Gilead? Is there no physician there? Why then is there no healing for the wound of My people?" (Jer. 8:22 NIV) We too must remind ourselves that we have the gift of healing, which has already been made available for us.

Yes, there are times when I feel lonely and need a physical touch. But, I know that these feelings are okay because they remind me that I am human, and that I feel this way because I need to snuggle up and worship the Father. After all, I am only a human being created by a loving God, a loving God who cannot wait to comfort me when I hurt. During these times I totally focus on the Lord. "Lord, are You there?" I often ask. Then I feel a calm reassurance in my heart, which reminds me that if His eyes are on the sparrow, He is most definitely watching over me (see Mt. 10:29).

The Lord showed me how to stand firm in his liberty. I remained free and healed that day. Thank you, Lord Jesus! The Lord showed me that healing and wholeness are one. We will never be healed until we have been made totally whole in the Lord Jesus Christ. I have come to realize, however, that wholeness and healing must take place daily the same way that we take up our cross daily as we deny ourselves. Just as my pain may come and go, I have realized that the pain is here today because I need to snuggle closer to Jesus and worship the Father so that He may be manifested stronger than ever. I need to know that He is there! I need to be able to cry, "Abba Father!" I need to sense the balm of His liquid love.

God Is in Control

On another day, I felt totally free from all my burdens, just joyful in the Lord. There were no cares. I was happy to be alive and serving the Lord!

It was the first day of school for Tesa as she entered the fifth grade at a new school. Tesa had progressed into the competitive level of gymnastics, and she worked out in the gym an average of 12 hours a week. After practice, I found out that Tesa had left her school books in her Uncle Junie's car, and of course, she had tons of homework. (Her uncle picks her up from school and takes her to the gym.) When I found out that Tesa had a lot of homework and books to cover, I became a little nervous because her bedtime was at 9:45 p.m. However, my brother was not due home until 10:45 p.m. I did not know what to do.

I started to reflect on the fact that God had helped me in my responsibilities as a single mother for almost five years. Although life had been good most of the time, there were times when I became panicky and nervous when things were even slightly out of order. I knew that I had to come up with a plan that night so that things would run smoothly again.

The plan was to awaken at 6:45 a.m. and have Tesa finish all assignments and place the protective coverings on each of her ten textbooks before school started. So I went to bed that night knowing that it was all under control.

I awoke the next day ready to ace my morning duty and make sure that Tesa was prepared for school. The chore of covering Tesa's ten textbooks took a lot longer than anticipated, so I started to panic again. I felt as though Tesa would be tagged as a slothful student by her teacher if she did not complete this simple assignment. You see, I felt everything had to be perfect in our lives and that we had no room for errors or mistakes. We had to manage our time wisely.

I had become a perfectionist after experiencing many trials. Part of this personality developed in me because of the guilt I felt when my husband died. These guilty feelings often caused me to question myself. I often wondered, *What if I had been a better wife, and what if I had not worried about my husband so much?*

When I first gave my life to Jesus Christ, I learned that our fear activates evil because the devil uses fear to overcome us. I always felt that the devil tricked me into fearing the loss of Stu (what a burden to carry). I was determined not to let my inadequacies cause anymore catastrophes in my life ever again, so I became an instant perfectionist. But, I was still carrying this awesome burden. From time to time I would still feel really hurt. After all, it had been five years now, and I thought that it was due time for things to be perfect again. That day, those feelings of inadequacy started all over again.

At 8:00 a.m. I had only covered six books and Tesa's school started at 8:15 a.m. I began to tell myself that I had plenty of time. Theoretically, we only lived five minutes from school if I drove 50 miles per hour and caught all the green traffic lights. I just knew I had the victory over this situation. I was determined to beat the clock by covering all of Tesa's books and still getting her to school on time.

When I realized that my plan was impossible, I questioned Tesa about the deadline for having the books covered. She told me that she did not think that all the books had to be covered today, but she was not quite sure of the due date. I thought she would make a good first impression if she met her first deadline or maybe beat the deadline. The clock was ticking away and I was still pushing it. The contact paper we used to cover the books ran out and we still had a couple of books left.

I immediately stopped, combed Tesa's hair, and left the house at 8:06 a.m., hoping to be at school before 8:15 a.m. When I caught the first red light, I began to panic. I knew that I had to make up for this lost time by driving faster. I was driving 45 miles per hour in a 30 mile per hour speed zone, and I was determined to start this day off right; if I didn't make my day right, no one else would do it for me.

Before I knew it, a police officer had pulled me aside for speeding. He told me that I had been driving 56 miles per hour in a 30 miles per hour zone, and I was shocked. The last time I had looked at my speedometer it had registered 45 miles per hour (still speeding of course, but not too bad). I immediately told the police officer that my daughter had to be at school on time. I even requested that the officer follow me to Tesa's school and write me the ticket after I had dropped her off so that she could still be early (I was obsessed with being perfect). Of course, he told me that my request was impossible so all I could do was sit there and wait.

At 8:12 a.m., we were still four miles away from school. We were late, of course, and Tesa began to cry.

This was her second day of school, and she was already tardy. I was extremely hurt because I knew that it was all my fault. The Lord had warned me by showing me the 30 mile per hour speed limit sign but *I was determined to use my own will and strength to accomplish my task.* These were the consequences of my self will:

Tesa was eight minutes late for school;

I had sinned by breaking the speed limit; and

I was stuck with a $45 speeding ticket as a result of my sin.

When I returned home, I wept frantically. I was angry and began to question God about the death of my husband. Why did Stu have to die anyway? "God, I can't do it all by myself!" I shouted. I pleaded to God for help. Then, a still voice said, "Jesus died so that you might have life." I cried it all out, and I realized that the Lord wanted me to rely totally on Him and not get caught up in all the tiny details of life. *He wanted me to relax and let Him take control.*

God wanted me to see that my strength would never be enough and that I had to depend on Him every step of the way. Finally, I came to grips with myself. I accepted the fact that today was not perfect from a humanistic standpoint, but it was perfect from God's perspective. He reminded me that I needed to remain humble and trust Him fully and there was no other way to serve Him.

God wanted me to lean on Him once more. I did just that and said, "Lord, take over the steering wheel again. I give up." At this point, I rejoiced because this day had brought me one step closer to God and one more step closer to total healing.

Make the Great Exchange

One day after I had helped a friend overcome a personal crisis, I received a revelation about standing firm in God's liberty. I had given all I had to help my friend through a personal crisis, but this friend had not shown any appreciation in return. I felt a lot of self-pity when this friend failed to recognize what I had done. At that moment, I began to reflect on the time of my husband's death, and I realized that most of the sadness I felt when he died had come from the fact that I felt betrayed and abandoned.

I remembered the anger I had felt because my husband had left my daughter and me all by ourselves, and I just knew that we could not possibly survive this life on our own. During that time, I cried uncontrollably because I was extremely fearful of facing every day by *myself.*

I began to compare my past hurt with this present hurt about my friend, and I realized that my hurt was only self-pity. At that instance, the Spirit of the Lord said, "I am here for you; I am the One who rewards you." Then, I remembered that the Lord never leaves me, even during those times when I act out of character. At that moment I made a decision to refuse to allow mere circumstances to overtake my emotions. That day

I chose to give my emotions to the Lord and have Him reign over them. I learned that only through this exchange of my emotions to the Master, was I able to move one step closer to total healing and total liberty from my hurts.

Selah

During the stages of our healing, we will go through some trying times, but we need not let those times get the best of us. During our difficult times we can learn to stand firm in Christ and make the great exchange of the difficult times for times of joy. During the difficult times the Father wants us to take:

...Beauty for ashes, the oil of joy for mourning, [and] *the garment of praise for the spirit of heaviness* (Isaiah 61:3a KJV).

Don't superficially pour on the oil of joy, or temporarily put on the garment of praise—make the great exchange! After we make these great exchanges, we can then be called oaks of righteousness, a planting of the Lord for His splendor. In other words, we will be planted strong and magnificent, distinguished for uprightness (like the palm tree), and be in right standing with God, so that God will be glorified (see Is. 61:3b). So make the great exchange and stand firm in it!

These events were all necessary for me to learn how to *stand firm in Christ.* We can only stand firm in His liberty when we totally let go and let Him lead every step of the way. Of course, this may be uncomfortable for most of us because we become so accustomed to doing things our way and feeling the way we want to when we want to. Nevertheless, letting go is the only way to fully stabilize our lives; for when we are weak, then we are strong! Therefore, let us put our total trust and confidence in the Lord so that we will be like a tree planted by the water.

If you do go through emotional periods of instability, my prayer is that you will rest in God and allow Him to take you through. There is always a lesson to be learned during these difficult times. So just proceed through those times knowing that joy awaits you at the end!

Chapter 10

Moving Ahead in Faith

All right! *We are standing firm.* Remember, we stand firm by exchanging our times of instability for times of joy. We take every experience in our lives and learn from it.

A Time to Review

In the beginning of this book, we had to place our "car" in the park mode (see Chapter 2). Now that we are standing firm, let's put our cars in drive again. *We are the only ones who can put our cars in the drive mode. However, in order to move ahead, we must continue to let God do the actual driving. Remember, He is the only fuel source that will last.* Are you ready to move ahead?

In the previous chapters, I told the tragic story that brought me to a saving knowledge of Jesus Christ. (Even though I received Him as Savior, I did not have a *knowledge* of Him. I had not accepted His promises for my life and I needed to allow Him to reign in my life.) I also told of my struggle to overcome my pain without confronting the real issue. When I finally defined and confronted my pain and its sinful consequences, my struggle ended in total humility and the fear of the Lord, which brought about true wisdom and a knowledge of God.

I also discussed the importance of learning who God is to us and abiding in Him on a daily basis. Finally, I told you how I was able to stand firm in His liberty after I recognized and accepted the fact that I serve an awesome, omnipotent God who stays with me every step of the way. I believe that every "widowhood" situation we face takes us through all or most of these phases until we learn to totally let go of ourselves and let God take full control.

Moving Ahead

In order to move ahead we must always keep these simple principles before us:

1. *We must continue to desire progress and not become entangled with perfection.*

Our humanity will always get in the way and make us think that success can be flawlessly achieved. Even the apostle Paul struggled, but he admitted to the importance of not having any confidence in the flesh. Paul said in Philippians 3:7-15:

> *But whatever was to my profit I now consider loss for the sake of Christ. What is more, I consider everything a loss compared to the surpassing greatness of knowing Christ Jesus my Lord, for whose sake I have lost all*

things. I consider them rubbish, that I may gain Christ and be found in Him, not having a righteousness of my own that comes from the law, but that which is through faith in Christ—the righteousness that comes from God and is by faith. **I want to know Christ and the power of His resurrection and the fellowship of sharing in His sufferings, becoming like Him in His death, and so, somehow, to attain to the resurrection from the dead. Not that I have already obtained all this, or have already been made perfect, but I press on to take hold of that for which Christ Jesus took hold of me. Brothers, I do not consider myself yet to have taken hold of it. But one thing I do: Forgetting what is behind and straining toward what is ahead, I press on toward the goal to win the prize for which God has called me heavenward in Christ Jesus** (Philippians 3:7-14 NIV).

2. *Know that the past is over and leave it there.*

If and when we fail in this healing process, we are to learn from those areas of defeat and move ahead. Also, even when we have progressed and overcome many of our hurts, we should not live in those achievements because this too will stunt us from moving ahead. Remember the apostle Paul said, "...*But one thing I do: Forgetting what is behind and straining toward what is ahead*" (Phil. 3:13 NIV).

3. *Hold onto the hope of the future and reach for it.*

...Press on toward the goal to win the prize for which God has called [you] *heavenward...* (Philippians 3:14).

We must recognize that our healing is a process. Also, it is important to strive for progress with the realization that, as humans, what we perceive as excellence may never be achieved. Instead, we are to continually make progress toward the end. We must always remind ourselves that the past is over and leave it there because we can only live in the present. Finally, know that the future holds hope. If you are established in the Lord Jesus Christ, press on toward the goal to win the prize!

Fight the Good Fight

I now acknowledge the fact that there may be many times when I feel tired and uninspired—like a soldier completing battle. These feelings are okay because life is indeed a battle field. *I must fight every battle until it is won and until my territory has been reclaimed and occupied for God.* It is quite evident that the adversary roams about the world seeking whom he may devour, and his sole mission is to kill, steal, and destroy. But the Lord is God and His grace is sufficient for me. That same grace is also available for you too.

The Lord Is Our Shepherd

During my healing, I learned the true meaning of Psalm 23. The Lord is my Shepherd (my Driver, Captain, Pilot, Overseer, always there to feed, guide, and shield me) I shall never want, for my God makes me to lie down in green pastures (only the fertile ground comes from God). He leadeth me beside the still waters. (The still waters represent total peace, the peace that "passeth all understanding" [see Phil. 4:7]. The world cannot give this peace, so we should never let the world attempt to take it away). He leads me in the paths of righteousness for His name's sake. (I do not deserve the Lord's blessings because my human nature is so sinful, and in my flesh dwells no good thing. I cannot continue to sin because I have realized that I cannot make it without God. God, I know that you forgive me for your glory—so that your name may be known to all men. God, I am here on this earth on your account). So, even though I walk through the valley of the shadow of death, I will fear no evil, for God is with me. (See Psalm 23.)

There will be tough times ahead. Yes, there will be times when you may hate the fact that you were left alone by your loved one, or perhaps, that you lack self-esteem, integrity, peace, right standing with God, or whatever your widowhood state may be. There are even times when the devil will put forth an all out attack to destroy you. But, I believe this is because the devil knows that if you let God totally heal you and use you for His glory, many lives will truly be touched and changed.

When we lose a loved one or we hurt from some other devastation in our lives, we may think that no one else understands. Therefore, we tend to listen to or seek counsel from only those who have had a similar loss or problem in their lives. That is why the devil wants to keep you from receiving your healing; there are only a few individuals who have been healed and are offering true godly advice on how to be healed from the death of a loved one or from other failures. *The Lord needs us. Be healed young widow and let the Lord do a mighty work in you! His rod and His staff will comfort you and surely His goodness and mercies will follow you all the days of your life and you will dwell in the house of the Lord forever!* (see Psalm 23)

Thanksgiving and Praise

I can genuinely say that the Lord has blessed my daughter and me in tremendous ways. He has blessed our relationship, and our love, as mother and daughter, has grown consistently over the years. God has blessed me with a wise child who adds a tremendous balance to my life. Although Tesa experienced great loss at the age of 4, God used her over and over to bring me joy and enthusiasm for life. We have a true knowledge of God, wisdom, patience, kindness, longsuffering, joy, peace, and love. All of these wonderful gifts are a result of the state of humility that we have been living in. The Lord has given me discernment and the ability to hear His still voice. His Spirit guides me even when my flesh does not understand.

Many parts of this book were written as a result of the Holy Spirit's moving and leading me to write. God often told me, *My child you need to share the blessings that I have bestowed upon you. When I told you to write this book, you had no idea how it would be done. But, this book will be written in My time as you allow yourself to listen and be guided by Me.* If you let God take control I mean total control—even when you are afraid—He will do some awesome works in your life.

Several chapters of this book were written when my natural man felt helpless and weak. Then the Lord said, *Let Me drive; let Me be Pilot, Captain, President, Overseer. My child, let Me lead.* Oh how beautiful it is to know that my God is Captain! Making God your Captain is the most beautiful feeling anyone can experience. His grace is truly sufficient for each of us! I know what it is to be in need, and I know what it is to have plenty. I have learned the secret of being content in any and every situation, whether well fed or hungry, whether living in plenty or in want. I can do and will do everything through Jesus Christ who gives me strength! (See Philippians 4:11-13 [NIV].) I am sufficient in Christ's sufficiency!! Hallelujah!

One Step at a Time

In summary, we need to take each step one at a time, one day at a time, and know that God's mercy and grace are provided for us every day. God never leaves us nor forsakes us. If you get tired, or even lonely, He is all you need, and He wants you to know that you do not have to fear because He is there. If God is to be Lord over our lives, our trials are necessary. In order to make Him Lord, we have to need Him. It is essential that we acknowledge and accept the fact that we have a Creator and a Savior in whom we live and move and have our entire being (see Acts 17:28). We must live in Him and move in Him daily because there is no other way. Remember, when we are weak then God is strong in us.

My God is awesome! Yes, He is awesome indeed, and His grace is sufficient for me. He is also your God. Why not let His grace be sufficient for you too!

Selah

My prayer is that you have been touched by what you have read. I also pray that you will compare and relate your own situation to what I have presented and that you will allow yourself to receive the true healing virtues of God through His balm of liquid love.

When you receive God's love, you too will be healed like the woman who was once bent over in a crushed state. That woman allowed herself to go through the healing process after she became submerged in a state of gloom and darkness. As her healing progressed, she entered into dawn, and finally her light broke forth before her as the noon day (see Ps. 37:6 NIV)! By God's grace, she evolved into a state of *wholeness*! I was that woman. (See graphical representation on page 101.)

Now, I pray that you too can say the following prayer as I did when I journeyed into wholeness.

"God, I thank You for sending Your Son, Jesus Christ, to this earth so that we all may be healed and made whole. I thank You that my spirit, soul (mind, will, and intellect), and body have finally come into agreement with that awesome event that took place at Calvary approximately 2,000 years ago. I thank You that I have now entered Your rest. Lord Jesus, I thank You for going all the way to the cross so that I might be healed. It is so wonderful to know You, Lord. It is so beautiful to be close to You. You are my Lord and my God. I love You. Yes, I love You, and I thank You for Jesus and the Holy Spirit, who dwells deep within me.

Lord, You are God; You are lovely; and You are worthy to be praised. Lord, I now know more than ever before that I will never make it without you."

Afterword

The Healing of a Widow

A Tribute to
Traditional Widows

*The Lord tears down the house of the proud, but He
makes secure the boundaries of the [consecrated] widow*
(Proverbs 15:25 AMP).

Widows, I challenge you to be courageous and
boldly take the journey into wholeness. If you are com-
mitted to take this journey, you too must be extremely
honest about all your emotional pain and confront the
true feelings that are deeply rooted within you. It is imperative that you take the time to explore your
thoughts so that all your hurts can come to the surface.
I sense your pain, and I know that it hurts because I
have been there.

However, I do know that we cannot allow ourselves
to be overcome by the pain. During our times of distress, it is extremely important that we allow ourselves
to remain alert and analytical about our feelings. Re-
maining alert and analytical sometimes require a daily

search deep within ourselves. After our feelings are defined and confronted, we must put aside our pride and humble ourselves before God. Humbling ourselves can bring exciting rewards because God promises to make secure the boundaries of the [consecrated] widow (see Prov. 15:25 AMP).

Only the truthful uncompromising reality of suffering a loss has been related in the previous chapters. Therefore, I will continually speak from that perspective. Only a bold and truthful confrontation with our hurts will bring about complete healing. After my own loss, I personally observed the lives of other widows who tried to prove to the world that their crisis was not so tragic and that they were immediately healed and strong enough to handle their predicament.

These women exhausted all of their energies concealing their true feelings and trying to keep their artificial happy faces in position. Some of these women became busybodies and overloaded their lives with many activities in an attempt to cloud their minds from the real pain. Other widows fluctuated in and out of unstable relationships, while still others isolated themselves from the world and became frustrated and embittered about their lives. (As I have admitted in earlier chapters, I possessed many of these characteristics before being healed.)

The Bible also speaks of the diverse characteristics of widows in First Timothy:

No widow may be put on the list of widows unless she is over sixty, has been faithful to her husband, and is well known for her good deeds, such as bringing up children, showing hospitality, washing the feet of the saints, helping those in trouble and devoting herself to all kinds of good deeds (1 Timothy 5:9-10 NIV).

Here, Paul advised the church to provide a place of refuge, in the natural, for widows over 60 who had proven to be faithful throughout their lives and to those widows who were truly dependent. On the contrary, in the next few verses Paul spoke of younger widows and he instructed women who were believers to help these widows.

As for younger widows, do not put them on such a list. For when their sensual desires overcome their dedication to Christ, they want to marry. Thus they bring judgment on themselves, because they have broken their first pledge. Besides, they get into the habit of being idle and going about from house to house. And not only do they become idlers, but also gossips and busybodies, saying things they ought not to. So I counsel younger widows to marry, to have children, to manage their homes and to give the enemy no opportunity for slander...If any woman who is a believer has widows in her family, she should help them and not let the church be burdened with them, so that the church can help those widows who are really in need (1 Timothy 5:11-16).

Although Paul spoke from a practical point of view, he knew that this was not God's best for younger widows. Paul merely gave a realistic suggestion to the church to deal with younger widows. His suggestion advised relatives to relieve the church from the burden posed by younger widows. Paul knew that younger widows were more vulnerable to the enemy's attacks because of their youthful energies and sensual desires. Therefore, he tried to provide the appropriate type of counsel that would protect these widows. He counseled younger widows to marry, have a family, and attend to their homes so that they would not bring slander to themselves.

Nevertheless, I believe that it is God's best to restore wholeness to our lives before we ever consider new relationships or families. Without a state of wholeness, we will never be satisfied with our lives, and we will only bring confusion to the lives of others. Additionally, each pain that is not confronted and dealt with leads to further chaos. For this reason, God has led me to speak directly to younger widows.

Although First Timothy 5:11-14 states that our sensual desires may overpower other decisions that we make, I do not believe that Jesus Christ wants us (younger widows) to break our original pledge with Him, regardless of our innate sensuality. Furthermore, He does not want us to go one more day without making and keeping our pledge to Him. This is the very pledge that we need to remain victorious over our hurts and to find and maintain our peace during this time of despair.

First Corinthians 15:57 says: "But thanks be to God! He gives us the victory through our Lord Jesus Christ"

(NIV). After being widowed at age 23, and after observing the lives of other widows, I have come to believe that younger widows are more vulnerable during their time of loss. Although our vulnerability is magnified by our youthful energies and sensual desires, we cannot afford to remain broken and divided. Our sufferings cause us to be divided by our pain and anything that is divided cannot stand as a whole unit. Therefore, this is not the time to merely *cope* with your hurts. As a widow, healing is not an option but a necessity for your survival. God's Word contains many promises for widows. Isaiah 54:4-7 (NIV) states:

> *"Do not be afraid; you will not suffer shame. Do not fear disgrace; you will not be humiliated. You will forget the shame of your youth and remember no more the reproach of your widowhood. For your Maker is your husband—the Lord Almighty is His name—the Holy One of Israel is Your Redeemer; He is called the God of all the earth. The Lord will call you back as if you were a wife deserted and distressed in spirit—a wife who married young, only to be rejected," says your God. "For a brief moment I abandoned you, but with deep compassion I will bring you back."*

The Bible also has other exciting promises for widows. For example, Psalm 146:9 (AMP) states that God upholds widows and sets them upright and Psalm 68:5 (NIV) states that God is a defender of widows. Also, in Acts Chapter 6, the ministry of Jesus' apostles were interrupted until they could specifically provide aid to the widows who were in need.

If you have not previously accepted the invitation to receive Jesus Christ in your life, I now offer you another opportunity. Isaiah 54 clearly states that the Holy One of Israel is your Redeemer, and He is called the God of all the earth. To receive Christ, make a confession that Jesus is Lord and believe in your heart that God raised Him from the dead. (See Romans 10:9-10.)

By now you should know that God specifically and uniquely cares about widows. Because God cares, He will ensure that we are completely healed from our state of widowhood. Therefore, let us travel through the healing process and explore some other characteristics that are uniquely relevant to us.

Let's begin by exploring some of the emotional feelings we experience during this time. As a young widow, I experienced many emotions like those you are probably experiencing right now. I understand the numbness caused by the immeasurable pain, the emptiness and loneliness (caused by the tearing apart of the deep love you mutually shared with your spouse), the anger you sometimes feel, and the helplessness and dismay you feel about your life after this loss. I understand the moments you awaken with a hope that your nightmare will soon end, only to realize that this tragedy is not a dream.

Also, there are times when you press on daily in a listless strength and return to a pillow, which is soon to be soaked with tears during the night. Furthermore, life becomes even more complicated for those of us who are left with children. We immediately sense the extra burden of singly rearing our children. Our lives literally take on the nature of a juggling act, with no allowances for errors.

As widows, we also suffer many other losses, and some of these losses are not always obvious; not only do we lose our husbands, but we also suffer the loss of self-esteem, peace, joy, and happiness. We may also lose the desire to cater to ourselves and sometimes our loss causes us to also compromise our principles, which ultimately leads to the loss of our integrity or perhaps our right standing with God.

To step further into the healing process, I suggest that you analyze a few of the key words used to define our feelings: *Numbness, emptiness, loneliness, helplessness, dismay, burdensome, juggling, self-esteem, peace, joy,* and *integrity.* Use your dictionary or thesaurus to research each word. As you read the respective definitions, think about your own feelings. Write down your feelings that are associated with each word in your notebook. This may seem futile; however, it is the biggest step toward confronting your true feelings. Add to the list words from your own experience and feelings.

If you have children, think about your role as a single mother. Have you tried to take on a dual role of father and mother? If so, you have just added another obstacle to becoming whole. During my healing process, God revealed to me that my only role in my daughter's life was to be her mother. This revelation removed a heavy burden from my life and moved me closer to wholeness. Yes, all we can be to our children is *mother* because God created us female. After receiving this revelation, I have literally seen the difference in the relationship with my daughter Tesa. Although I have always loved Tesa dearly, I often added extra pressure to her life by trying to carry out the dual role of mother and father. Daily, I fruitlessly struggled to be what I could never be. Now, Tesa and I share many more intimate times as mother and daughter. As a result, our love for each other has grown tremendously. We have also become better friends since I now place all my energies into relating to her from a motherly perspective. If you are concerned about a male influence in the lives of your children, consider the men in your family or the men in your neighborhood churches; and, of course, consistently pray that God will send good male role models to your children.

Now that you have explored and analyzed some of your unique characteristics and emotions, ask God to heal you from all negative feelings and fears. Next, ask God to heal you from the memories of these feelings and fears. Finally, ask God to give you the miracle to live your life as if you had never experienced these feelings or fears.

Of course, there is no magic to this, but the key is to confront your pain, humble yourself, and then make God personal to your situation. If negative feelings try to return, then stand firm in the liberty that God has already given you, move ahead daily—pressing on toward the mark of complete wholeness.

Young widow, always remember that you are not alone. Although you have asked, "Why me?" over and over, many other women are experiencing the same perplexity. However, you can be completely freed from your distress, just as I have been freed. You too can exchange that deep, intimate hurt, that is often difficult to express, for a refreshed life of wholeness–one filled with peace, joy, and new energies; one unhindered by your past.

I want to encourage you to seek the Kingdom of God and all His righteousness on a daily basis (see Mt. 6:33). As you continually do this, you will receive total peace; the peace that transcends all understanding and which guards your hearts and minds (Phil. 4:7). Allow God Himself, the God of peace, to sanctify you through and through. He is the One who called us. He is faithful and He will do it. (See First Thessalonians 5:23-24 NIV.)

As you receive peace, the type of peace that the world cannot give you, you will then begin to experience an outpouring of the *oil of joy* instead of mourning (see Is. 61:3). This joy will be your strength (see Neh. 8:10)! You will be restored with a new love for yourself and a renewed love for others. You will experience a life filled with the sufficiency of the Lord Jesus Christ.

Finally, you will experience a life where you have entered into the rest that God has provided for you through His Son Jesus Christ.

So then, there is still awaiting a full and complete Sabbath-rest reserved for the [true] people of God; for he who has once entered [God's] rest also has ceased from [the weariness and pain] of human labors, just as God rested from those labors peculiarly His own. Let us therefore be zealous and exert ourselves and strive diligently to enter into that rest [of God, to know and to experience it for ourselves]... (Hebrews 4:9-11 AMP).

Letters of Testimony and Encouragement

Dear Sister Dorn:

I want to praise and thank our heavenly Father for blessing and allowing me to come across your path. You have been an awesome blessing to me in this life and have truly used your gift of exhortation in the times that I felt deep pain and suffering. You will never know how much this has meant to me and to our heavenly Father. I thank you for your example of love for the Body of Christ and the lost. God said in His Word, "Anyone who does not love his brother whom he has seen, cannot love God, whom he has not seen" (see 1 Jn. 4:20). I love you, Dorn.

Thank you so much for the encouragement, the "oil of joy," and the "garment of praise" instead of the spirit of heaviness (Is. 6:3). Hallelujah!

Healed and in His Purpose,
Your Sister in Christ

This individual was extremely despondent and depressed for many years, but now lives a happy fulfilled life.

Dorn,

Thank you for your prayers and words of encouragement. I've read your letter over and over. It gives me some consolation over the loss of my husband.

Yours in Christ

Dorn,

Only a few minutes ago, I read that letter you wrote me over a year ago. Each time I read it, I'm encouraged by it. It is a beautiful letter!! Dorn, although a year has passed since my husband's death, not a day goes by that I don't think of him. Each day brings about a new experience. But, with each experience I am guided and sustained by my Father God because Jesus Christ abides in me....

Yours in Christ

This third individual lost her husband in 1993, and she now realizes that God wants her healed from this state of brokenness.

God is no respecter of persons. ***Women, let us give birth to wholeness! Woe unto us if we remain with child. Let us give birth so that we can exemplify wholeness to our families, and ultimately wholeness to the world!***

It is the Father who consoled, comforted, and encouraged me during this time of trouble. Therefore, I know that it is the Father's will for me to use this comfort to console those who are in this same situation.

If you have received Jesus Christ as your personal Savior through the reading of this book, or if you have experienced a healing from the brokenness in your life, I would like to hear from you. Please write to me. I would like to send you some additional material to assist you in your new life in Christ.

Write to:
Dorn J.B. Wheatley
(d/b/a) Kingdom Lifestyle, Inc.
P.O. Box 4193
Capitol Heights, MD 20791-4193

Order Form

(Photocopy for additional orders)

Quantity	Price	Total
Subtotal		
5% Sales Tax (Maryland only)		
$2.00 postage/handling		
TOTAL		

Name _____

Address _____

City _____ State _____ Zip _____

For scheduling motivational seminars, workshops, retreats, or meetings with Dorn J.B. Wheatley contact:

Oil of Joy Ministry
(d/b/a) Kingdom Lifestyle, Inc.
P.O. Box 4193
Capitol Heights, Maryland 20791-4193

To order toll free call:
1-800-722-6774

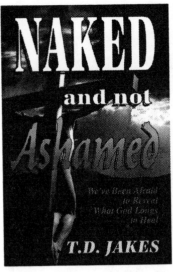

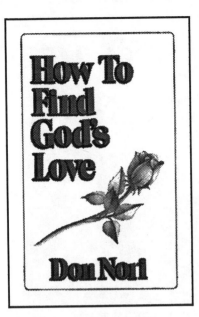

HOW TO FIND GOD'S LOVE

by Don Nori.

Here is a heartwarming story about three people who tell their stories of tragedy, fear, and disease, and how God showed them His love in a real way.

TPB-108p. ISBN 0-914903-28-4

Retail $3.99

(4¼" X 7")

Also available in Spanish.

TPB-144p. ISBN 1-56043-024-9

Retail $3.99

(4¼" X 7")